1001nights

Illustrated Fairy Tales from One Thousand and One Nights

Contents

8

Aladdin and the Wonderful Lamp

Illustrated by Catalina Estrada Uribe

There once lived a poor tailor, who had a son called Aladdin, a careless, idle boy who would do nothing but play all day long in the streets with little idle boys like himself. When he reached his tenth year, his father decided to teach him his own trade, and he took Aladdin into his shop that he might be taught tailoring. But, as Aladdin was a careless, idle boy, who only wanted to play at all times with the gutter boys of the quarter, he would not sit in the shop for a single day. This so grieved his father that he died, yet, in spite of his mother's tears and prayers, Aladdin did not mend his ways. One day, when he was playing in the streets as usual, a stranger asked him his age and if he were not the son of Mustapha the tailor.

"I am, Sir," replied Aladdin, "but he died a long while ago."

On this the stranger, who was a famous African magician, fell on his neck and kissed him, saying, "I am your uncle and knew you from your likeness to my brother. Go to your mother and tell her I am coming." So saying, the magician put hand to purse, and pulling out ten gold pieces, gave them to the lad, "O my son, take this money and give it to thy mother, greeting her from me, and let her know that your uncle, thy father's brother, hath reappeared from his exile and that tomorrow I will visit her to salute her with the salaam and see the house wherein my brother was homed and look upon the place where he lieth buried." Aladdin ran home and told his mother of his newly found uncle.

"Indeed, child," she said, "your father had a brother, but I always thought he was dead." However, she prepared supper and bade Aladdin to seek his uncle, but the magician beguiled him with pleasant stories and led him on in spite of himself.

At last they came to two mountains divided by a narrow valley.

"We will go no further," said the false uncle. "I will show you something wonderful, you gather up sticks while I kindle a fire."

Once it was lit the magician threw on it a little powder he had about him, at the same time saying some magical words. The earth trembled a little and opened in front of them, disclosing a square flat stone with a brass ring in the middle to raise it by. Aladdin tried to run away, but the magician caught him and gave him a blow that knocked him down. "What have I done, uncle?" he said piteously, whereupon the magician said more kindly, "Fear nothing, but obey me. Beneath this stone lies a treasure which is to be yours and no one else may touch it, so set thy hand upon the ring and raise the stone, for that none other amongst the people, thyself excepted, hath power to open it, nor may any of mortal birth save thyself set foot within this enchanted treasury which hath been kept for thee." At the word treasure, Aladdin forgot his fears and grasped the ring as he was told, saying the names of his father and grandfather. The stone came up quite easily and some steps appeared.

"Go down," said the magician, "at the foot of these steps you will find an open door leading into three large halls. In each of these thou shalt see four golden jars and others of silver. However, beware lest thou touch them, nor allow thy gown or its skirts even to brush the jars or the walls. Leave them and fare forward without lingering for a single moment on the way. And if thou do anything contrary thereto, thou wilt at once be transformed and become a black stone. These halls lead into a garden of fine fruit trees. Walk on until you come to a niche in a terrace where stands a lighted lamp. Pour out the oil it contains and bring it to me. And on return thou art allowed to pluck from the trees what thou wishes, for all is thine so long as the lamp is in thy hand."

He drew a ring from his finger and gave it to Aladdin, saying, "This ring shall free thee from all hurt and fear which may threaten thee, but only on condition that thou bear in mind all I have told thee. So arise straightway and go down the steps, strengthening thy purpose and girding the loins of resolution. Moreover, fear not, for thou art now a man and no longer a child. And in shortest time, O my son, thou shalt possess immense riches and thou shalt become the wealthiest of the world."

Aladdin found everything as the magician had said, gathered some fruit off the trees and, having got the lamp, arrived at the mouth of the cave. The magician cried out in a great hurry, "Make haste and give me the lamp." This Aladdin refused to do until he was out of the cave. The magician flew into a terrible passion and throwing some more powder on the fire, he said something and the stone rolled back into its place, and Aladdin, unable to issue forth, remained underground.

The magician left Persia for ever, which plainly showed that he was no uncle of Aladdin's, but a cunning magician who had read in his magic books of a wonderful lamp, which would make him the most powerful man in the world. Though he alone knew where to find it, he could only receive it from the hand of another. He had picked out the foolish Aladdin for this purpose, intending to get the lamp and kill him afterwards.

For two days Aladdin remained in the dark, crying and shouting to the magician, whom he believed to be his uncle, and praying him to lend a hand that he might issue from the ground and return to earth's surface. But however loudly he cried, none was found to reply. At last he clasped his hands in prayer and in so doing rubbed the ring, which the magician had forgotten to take from him. Immediately an enormous and frightful genie rose out of the earth, saying, "What wouldst thou with me? I am the Slave of the Ring and will obey thee in all things."

Aladdin trembled at the terrible sight, but fearlessly replied, "Deliver me from this place!" And hardly had he spoken this speech when suddenly the ground clave asunder and he found himself outside in full view of the world. Now for two whole days he had been sitting in the darkness of the treasury underground, and when the sheen of day and the shine of sun smote his face he found himself unable to keep his eyes open, but as soon as his eyes could bear the light he went home, but fainted on the threshold. When he came to himself he told his mother what had passed and showed her the lamp and the fruits he had gathered in the garden, which were in reality precious stones. He then asked for some food.

"Alas! child," she said, "I have nothing in the house, but I have spun a little cotton and will go and sell it."

Aladdin bade her to keep her cotton, for he would sell the lamp instead. As it was very dirty she began to rub it, that it might fetch a higher price. Instantly a hideous genie appeared and said, "Say what thou wantest of me. Here am I, thy slave and slave to whoso holdeth the lamp, and not I alone, but all the Slaves of the Wonderful Lamp which thou holdeth in thy hand." She fainted away, but Aladdin, snatching the lamp, said boldly, "Fetch me something to eat!"

The genie returned with a silver bowl, twelve silver plates containing rich meats, two silver cups and two bottles of wine. Aladdin's mother, when she came to herself, said, "Whence comes this splendid feast?"

"Ask not, but eat," replied Aladdin.

So they sat at breakfast until it was dinner-time and Aladdin told his mother about the lamp. She begged him to sell it and have nothing to do with devils.

"No," said Aladdin, "since chance has made us aware of its virtues, we will use it and the ring likewise, which I shall always wear on my finger." When they had eaten all the genie had brought, Aladdin sold one of the silver plates and so on until none were left. He then had recourse to the genie, who gave him another set of plates and thus they lived for many years.

One day Aladdin heard an order from the Sultan which proclaimed that everyone was to stay at home and close their shutters while the princess, his daughter, went to and from the bath. Aladdin was seized by a desire to see her face, which was very difficult, as she always went veiled. He hid himself behind the door of the bath and peeped through a chink. Now after the Sultan's daughter had gone the rounds of the city and its main streets and had solaced herself by sight-seeing, she finally reached the bath, and whilst entering lifted her veil and looked so beautiful that Aladdin fell in love with her at first sight. He went home so changed that his mother was frightened. He told her he loved the princess so deeply that he could not live without her and meant to ask her in mar-

13

riage of her father. His mother, on hearing this, burst out laughing, but Aladdin at last
prevailed upon her to go before the Sultan and carry his request.

"In what way shall I ask the Sultan for his daughter to be thy wife, and indeed how ever
shall I even get access to him? And should I succeed therein, what is to be my answer
when they ask me about thy means? Haply the King will hold me to be a madwoman.
And lastly, suppose that I obtain audience of the Sultan, what offering is there I can sub-
mit to him?" Aladdin replied, "We have in our house a bowl of China porcelain, so arise
and fetch it, that I may fill it with jewels which thou shalt carry as a gift to the Sultan,
and thou shalt stand in his presence and solicit him for my requirement. I am certain
that by such means the matter will become easy to thee, and if thou be unwilling, O my
mother, to strive for the winning of my wish as regards the Sultan's daughter, know thou
that surely I shall die. Nor do thou imagine that this gift is of aught save the costliest
of stones, and be assured, O my mother, that in my many visits to the jewellers' bazaar
I have observed the merchants selling for sums man's judgment may not determine
jewels whose beauty is not worth one quarter-carat of what we possess, seeing which I
was certified that ours are beyond all price. So arise, O my mother, as I bade thee, and

bring me the porcelain bowl aforesaid, that I may arrange therein some of these gems, and we will see what semblance they show."

She took these with her to please the Sultan and set out, trusting in the lamp. When she passed into the palace, the Levee not being fully attended, she saw the Grand-Vizir and the Lords of Council going into the presence room, and after a short time, when the Divan was made complete by the ministers and high officials and chieftains and Emirs and grandees, the Sultan appeared and seated himself upon his throne, and all present at the Levee stood before him with crossed arms awaiting his commandment to sit, and when they received it, each took his place accordingly. Aladdin's mother entered the hall and placed herself in front of the Sultan. He, however, took no notice of her. She went every day for a week and stood in the same place.

When the council broke up on the sixth day the Sultan said to his Grand-Vizir, "I see a certain woman in the audience-chamber every day carrying something in a porcelain bowl. Call her next time, so that I may find out what she wants."

Next day, at a sign from the Grand-Vizir, she went up to the foot of the throne and remained kneeling until the Sultan said to her, "Rise, good woman and tell me what you want."

She saluted the Sultan by kissing her finger tips and raising them to her brow, and, praying for the Sultan's glory and continuance and the permanence of his prosperity, and kissed the ground before him. Thereupon quoth he, "O woman, for sundry days I have seen thee attend the levee without a word said, so tell me have thou any requirement I may grant." She kissed the ground a second time, but hesitated, so the Sultan sent away all but the Grand-Vizir and bade her to speak freely, promising to forgive her beforehand for anything she might say. She then told him of her son's violent love for the princess. "I prayed him to forget her," she said, "but in vain, he threatened to do some desperate deed if I refused to go and ask your Majesty for the hand of the princess. Now I pray you to forgive not me alone, but also my son Aladdin."

The Sultan asked her kindly what she had in the porcelain bowl, whereupon she presented the jewels to him.

The audience hall was illumined as it were by lusters and candelabra. And the Sultan was dazed and amazed at the radiance of the rare gems, and he fell to marvelling at their size and beauty and excellence and cried, "Never have I seen anything like these jewels for size and beauty and excellence, nor deem I that there be found in my

Treasury a single one like them." He was thunderstruck and turning to the Grand-Vizir said, "What sayest thou? Tell me, hast thou seen in thy time such mighty fine jewels as these?"

The other answered, "Never have I seen such, O our lord the Sultan, nor do I think that there be in the treasures of my lord the Sultan a single one like them."

The Sultan resumed, "Ought I not to bestow the princess on one who values her at such a price?"

When the Grand-Vizir heard the Sultan's words, he was tongue-tied with concern, and he grieved with sore grief, for he wanted her for his own son. He begged the Sultan to withhold her for three months, during the course of which he hoped his son would contrive to make him a richer present. The Sultan granted this and told Aladdin's mother, "Go to thy son and tell him I have pledged my word that my daughter shall be in his name. Only it is needful that I make the requisite preparations of nuptial furniture for her use, and he should be patient for the next three months." Receiving this reply, Aladdin's mother thanked the Sultan and blessed him, then, going forth in hottest haste, as one flying for joy, she went home. And when her son saw her entering with a smiling face, he was gladdened, especially because she had returned without delay, as on the past days, and had not brought back the China porcelain bowl.

Aladdin waited patiently for nearly three months, but after two had elapsed his mother, going into the city to buy oil, found all the market shops fast shut and the whole city decorated and everyone rejoicing. She beheld the soldiers and household troops riding in procession, and she wondered at the marvellous sight and the glamour of the scene. So she went into a shop which still stood open and bought her oil and asked, "Tell me what be the tidings in town this day, that people have made all these decorations and every house and market street is adorned and the troops all stand on guard?"

"Do you not know," was the answer, "that the son of the Grand-Vizir is to marry the Sultan's daughter tonight?"

Breathless, she ran and told Aladdin, who was seized with a fever of jealousy, brought on by his grief, but presently bethought him of the lamp. He rubbed it and the genie appeared, saying, "What is thy will?"

Aladdin replied, "I prayed the Sultan for his daughter to wife and he plighted her to me after three months, but he hath not kept his word, no, he hath given her to the son of the Grand-Vizir, and this very night the bridegroom will go into her chamber. Therefore,

I command thee, when thou shalt see bride and bridegroom bedded together this night, at once take them up and bring them hither."

"Master, I obey," said the genie.

Aladdin then went to his chamber, where, sure enough at midnight the genie transported the bed containing the Grand-Vizir's son and the princess.

"Take this newly-married man," he said, "and put him outside in the cold and return at daybreak." Whereupon the genie took the Grand-Vizir's son out of the bed leaving Aladdin alone with the princess.

"Fear nothing," Aladdin said to her, "you are my wife, promised to me by your unjust father and no harm shall come to you."

The princess was too frightened to speak and passed the most miserable night of her life, while Aladdin lay down beside her and slept soundly. At the appointed hour the genie fetched in the shivering bridegroom, laid him in his place and transported the bed back to the palace. Presently the Sultan came to wish his daughter good-morning. The unhappy Grand-Vizir's son jumped up and hid himself, while the princess would not say a word and was very sorrowful.

The Sultan sent her mother to her, who said, "How comes it, child that you will not speak to your father? What has happened?"

The princess sighed deeply and related to her mother all that had befallen her that night, how they had taken away her bridegroom, leaving her lone and lonesome, and how after a while came another youth who lay beside her in lieu of her bridegroom, after placing his scimitar between her and himself.

"And in the morning," she continued, "he who carried us off returned and bore us straight back to our own stead. But at once when he arrived hither he left us, and suddenly my father, the Sultan, entered at the hour and moment of our coming and I had neither heart nor tongue to speak to him, for the stress of the terror and trembling which came upon me. Haply such lack of duty may have proved sore to him, so I hope, O my mother, that thou wilt acquaint him with the cause of this my condition, and pardon me for not answering him and blame me not, and accept my excuses." Her mother did not believe her in the least, but bade her to rise and consider it an idle dream.

The following night exactly the same thing happened and next morning, on the princess' refusing to speak, the Sultan threatened to cut off her head. She then confessed all, bidding him to ask the Grand-Vizir's son if it were not so. The Sultan told the Grand-Vizir to

ask his son, who owned the truth, adding that, dearly as he loved the princess, he would rather die than go through another such fearful and cold night and wished to be separated from her. His wish was granted and there was an end of feasting and rejoicing.

When the three months were over, Aladdin sent his mother to remind the Sultan of his promise. She stood in the same place as before and the Sultan, who had forgotten Aladdin, at once remembered him and sent for her. On seeing her poverty the Sultan felt less inclined than ever to keep his word and asked the Grand-Vizir's advice, who counselled him to set so high a value on the princess that no man living could come up to it.

The Sultan then turned to Aladdin's mother, saying, "Good woman, a Sultan must remember his promises and I will remember mine, but your son must first send me forty basins of gold brimful of jewels, carried by forty black slaves, led by as many white ones, splendidly dressed. Tell him that I await his answer." Aladdin's mother bowed low and went home, thinking all was lost.

She gave Aladdin the message, adding, "He may wait long enough for your answer!"

"Not so long, mother, as you think," her son replied, "I would do a great deal more than that for the princess."

Aladdin retired to his chamber and, taking the lamp, rubbed it and summoned the genie and in a few moments the eighty slaves arrived and filled up the small house and garden.

Aladdin made them set out to the palace, two and two, followed by his mother. And when the people sighted such a mighty fine sight and marvellous spectacle, all stood and stared and considered the forms and figures of the slaves, marvelling at their beauty and loveliness, for each and every wore robes inwrought with gold and studded with jewels, no dress being worth less than a thousand dinars. The people stared just as intently at the basins of gold they carried on their heads, and albeit these were covered with pieces of brocade dubbed with precious stones.

They entered the palace and set down from their heads the basins at the Sultan's feet and, having removed the brocade covers, stood in a half-circle around the throne with their arms crossed, while Aladdin's mother presented them to the Sultan.

The Sultan wondered with exceeding wonder and was distraught by the beauty of the slaves and their loveliness, which passed praise. And his wits were wildered when he considered the golden basins brimful of gems which captured his vision, and he was perplexed at the marvel until he became unable to utter a syllable for the excess of his wonder. Also his sense was stupefied even more when he considered that within an hour or so all these treasures had been collected. He hesitated no longer, but said, "Good woman, return and tell your son that I wait for him with open arms."

She lost no time in telling Aladdin, bidding him to make haste. But Aladdin first called the genie.

"I want a scented bath," he said, "a richly embroidered habit, a horse surpassing the Sultan's and twenty slaves to attend me. Besides this, six slaves, beautifully dressed, to wait on my mother, and lastly ten thousand pieces of gold in ten purses."

No sooner said than done. Aladdin mounted his horse and passed through the streets, the slaves strewing gold as they went. Those who had played with him in his childhood knew him not, he had grown so handsome.

When the Sultan saw Aladdin dressed in his princely suit he looked upon him and considered his beauty and loveliness. He also considered the eloquence of Aladdin and his delicacy of speech, and came down from his throne, embraced him and led him into a hall where a feast was spread, intending to marry him to the princess that very day. But Aladdin refused, saying, "I must build a palace fit for her," and took his leave.

Once home he said to the genie, "Build me a palace of the finest marble, set with jasper, agate and other precious stones. In the middle you shall build me a large hall with a dome, its four walls of massy gold and silver, each side having six windows, whose lattices, all except one, which is to be left unfinished, must be set with diamonds and rubies. There must be stables and horses and grooms and slaves, go and see about it!"

The palace was finished by the next day and the genie carried him there and showed him that all his orders had been faithfully carried out, even to the laying of a velvet carpet from Aladdin's palace to the Sultan's. Aladdin was awestruck and astounded by the magnificent display of wealth, which not even the mightiest monarch on earth could produce, and more so to see his palace fully provided with eunuchs and handmaids whose beauty was indescribable. Aladdin's mother then dressed herself carefully and walked to the palace with her slaves, while he followed her on horseback. The Sultan sent musicians with trumpets and cymbals to meet them, so that the air resounded with music and cheers. She was taken to the princess, who saluted her and treated her with great honour. At night the princess said goodbye to her father and set out on the carpet for Aladdin's palace, with his mother at her side and followed by the hundred slaves. She was charmed at the sight of Aladdin, who ran to receive her.

"Princess," he said, "blame your beauty for my boldness if I have displeased you."

She told him that, having seen him, she willingly obeyed her father in this matter. After the wedding had taken place Aladdin led her into the hall, where a feast was spread and she supped with him, after which they danced until midnight.

The next day Aladdin invited the Sultan to see the palace. On entering the hall with the four-and-twenty windows, with their rubies, diamonds and emeralds, he cried, "It is a world's wonder! There is only one thing that surprises me. Was it by accident that one window was left unfinished?"

"No, Sir, by design," returned Aladdin. "I wished your Majesty to have the glory of finishing this palace." The Sultan was pleased and sent for the best jewellers in the city. He showed them the unfinished window and bade them fit it up like the others.

"Sir," replied their spokesman, "we cannot find jewels enough."

The Sultan had his own fetched, which they soon used, but to no purpose, for in a month's time the work was not half done. Aladdin, knowing that their task was in vain, bade them to undo their work and carry the jewels back and the genie finished the window at his command. Then the jewellers went to the Sultan and told him of what Aladdin had bidden, so he asked them, "What said he to you, and what was his reason, and why was he not content that the window be finished and why did he undo your work?"

They answered, "We know not at all, but he bade us to deface what we had done."

Hereupon the Sultan at once called for his horse, and visited Aladdin, who showed him the window finished. The Sultan embraced him saying, "O my son, thou canst work in a single night what in a month the jewellers could not do. By Allah, I deem thou hast nor brother nor rival in this world." The envious Grand-Vizir meanwhile hinted that it was the work of enchantment.

Aladdin had won the hearts of the people by his gentle bearing. He was made captain of the Sultan's armies and won several battles for him, but remained modest and courteous as before and lived thus in peace and content for several years.

But far away in Africa the magician remembered Aladdin and by his magic arts discovered that Aladdin, instead of perishing miserably in the cave, had escaped and married a princess, with whom he was living in great honour and wealth. He knew that the poor tailor's son could only have accomplished this by means of the lamp and travelled night

24

and day until he reached the capital of China, bent on Aladdin's ruin. As he passed through the town he heard people talking everywhere about a marvellous palace.

"Forgive my ignorance," he asked, "what is this palace you speak of?"

"Have you not heard of Prince Aladdin's palace," was the reply, "the greatest wonder of the world? I will direct you if you have a mind to see it."

The magician thanked him who spoke and having seen the palace knew that it had been raised by the genie of the lamp and became half mad with rage. He was determined to get hold of the lamp and to again plunge Aladdin into the deepest poverty.

Unluckily, Aladdin had gone a-hunting for eight days, which gave the magician plenty of time. He bought a dozen copper lamps, put them into a basket and went to the palace, crying, "New lamps for old!" followed by a jeering crowd.

The princess, sitting in the hall of four-and-twenty windows, sent a slave to find out what the noise was about, who came back laughing, so that the princess scolded her.

"Madam," replied the slave, "who can help laughing to see an old fool offering to exchange fine new lamps for old ones?"

Another slave said, "There is an old one on the cornice there which he can have." Now this was the magic lamp, which Aladdin had left there, as he could not take it out hunting with him. The princess, not knowing its value, laughingly bade the slave to take it and make the exchange. She went and said to the magician, "Give me a new lamp for this." He snatched it and bade the slave to take her choice, amid the jeers of the crowd. Little he cared, but left off crying his lamps and went out of the city gates to a lonely place, where he remained until nightfall, when he pulled out the lamp and rubbed it. The genie appeared and at the magician's command carried him, together with the palace and the princess in it, to a lonely place in Africa.

The next morning the Sultan looked out of the window towards Aladdin's palace and rubbed his eyes, for it was gone. He sent for the Grand-Vizir and asked what had become of the palace. The Grand-Vizir looked out too and was lost in astonishment. He again put it down to enchantment and this time the Sultan believed him and sent thirty men on horseback to fetch Aladdin in chains. They met him riding home, bound him and forced him to go with them on foot. The people, however, who loved him, followed, armed, to see that he came to no harm. He was carried before the Sultan, who ordered the executioner to cut off his head. The executioner made Aladdin kneel down, bandaged his eyes and raised his scimitar to strike.

At that instant the Grand-Vizir, who saw that the crowd had forced their way into the courtyard and were scaling the walls to rescue Aladdin, called to the executioner to stay his hand. The people, indeed, looked so threatening that the Sultan gave way and ordered Aladdin to be unbound and pardoned him in the sight of the crowd. Aladdin now begged to know what he had done.

"False wretch!" said the Sultan, "come hither," and showed him from the window the place where his palace had stood. Aladdin was so amazed that he could not say a word. "Where are your palace and my daughter?" demanded the Sultan. "For the first I am not so deeply concerned, but my daughter I must have and you must find her or lose your head."

Aladdin begged for forty days in which to find her, promising that if he failed to return to suffer death at the Sultan's pleasure. His prayer was granted and he went forth sadly from the Sultan's presence. For three days he wandered about like a madman, asking everyone what had become of his palace, but they only laughed and pitied him. He came to the banks of a river and knelt down to say his prayers before throwing himself in. In so doing he rubbed the magic ring he still wore. The genie he had seen in the cave appeared and asked his will.

"Save my life, genie," said Aladdin, "and bring my palace back."

"That is not in my power," said the genie, "I am only the slave of the ring, you must ask the slave of the lamp."

"Even so," said Aladdin, "but thou canst take me to the palace and set me down under my dear wife's window." He at once found himself in Africa, under the window of the princess and fell asleep out of sheer weariness.

He was awakened by the singing of the birds and his heart was lighter. He saw plainly that all his misfortunes were owing to the loss of the lamp and vainly wondered who had robbed him of it.

That morning the princess rose earlier than she had done since she had been carried to Africa by the magician, whose company she was forced to endure once a day. She, however, treated him so harshly that he dared not live there altogether. As she was dressing, one of her women looked out and saw Aladdin. The princess ran and opened the window and at the noise she made Aladdin looked up. She called to him to come to her and great was the joy of these lovers at seeing each other again.

After he had kissed her Aladdin said, "I beg of you, Princess, in God's name, before we

speak of anything else, for your own sake and mine, tell me what has become of an old lamp I left on the cornice in the hall of four-and-twenty windows, when I went a-hunting."

"Alas!" she said "I am the innocent cause of our sorrows," and told him of the exchange of the lamp.

"Now I know," cried Aladdin, "that we have to thank the African magician for this! Where is the lamp?"

"He carries it about with him," said the princess, "I know, for he pulled it out of his breast to show me. He wishes me to break my faith with you and marry him, saying that you were beheaded by my father's command. He is forever speaking ill of you, but I only reply by my tears. If I persist, I doubt not that he will use violence." Aladdin comforted her and left her for a while. He changed clothes with the first person he met in the town and having bought a certain powder returned to the princess, who let him in by a little side door.

"Put on your most beautiful dress," he said to her, "and receive the magician with smiles, leading him to believe that you have forgotten me. Invite him to sup with you and say you wish to taste the wine of his country. He will go for some and while he is gone I will tell you what to do."

She listened carefully to Aladdin and when he left arrayed herself gaily for the first time since she had left China. She put on a girdle and head-dress of diamonds and seeing in a mirror that she looked more beautiful than ever, received the magician, saying to his great amazement, "I have made up my mind that Aladdin is dead and that all my tears will not bring him back to me, so I am resolved to mourn no more and have therefore invited you to sup with me, but I am tired of the wines of China and would like to taste those of Africa." The magician flew to his cellar and the princess put the powder Aladdin had given her in her cup. When he returned she asked him to drink to her health in the wine of Africa, handing him her cup in exchange for his as a sign she was reconciled to him. Before drinking the magician made her a speech in praise of her beauty, but the princess cut him short saying, "Let me drink first and you shall say what you will afterwards." She set her cup to her lips and kept it there, while the magician drained his to the dregs and fell back lifeless. The princess then opened the door to Aladdin and flung her arms round his neck, but Aladdin pushed her away, bidding her to leave him, as he had more to do. He then went to the dead magician, took the lamp out of his vest and bade the genie to carry the palace and all in it back to China. This was done and the princess in her chamber only felt two little shocks and without thought she was at home again.

The Sultan, who was sitting in his closet, mourning for his lost daughter, happened to look up and rubbed his eyes, for there stood the palace as before! He hastened thither and Aladdin received him in the hall of the four-and-twenty windows, with the princess at his side. Aladdin told him what had happened and showed him the dead body of the magician, so that he might believe. A ten days' feast was proclaimed and it seemed as if Aladdin might now live the rest of his life in peace, but it was not to be.

The African magician had a younger brother, who was, if possible, even more wicked and even more cunning than himself. He travelled to China to avenge his brother's death and went to visit a pious woman called Fatima, thinking she might be of use to him. He entered her cell and clapped a dagger to her breast, telling her to rise and do his bidding on pain of death. He changed clothes with her, coloured his face like hers, put on her veil and murdered her, so that she might tell no tales. Then he went towards the palace of Aladdin and all the people thinking he was the holy woman, gathered round him, kissing his hands and begging his blessing. When he got to the palace there

30

was such a noise going on round him that the princess bade her slave to look out of the window and to ask what was the matter. The slave said it was the holy woman, curing people by her touch of their ailments, whereupon the princess, who had long desired to see Fatima, sent for her. On coming to the princess the magician offered up a prayer for her health and prosperity. When he had done the princess made him sit by her and begged him to stay with her always. The false Fatima, who wished for nothing better, consented, but kept his veil down for fear of discovery. The princess showed him the hall and asked him what he thought of it.

"It is truly beautiful," said the false Fatima. "In my mind it wants but one thing."

"And what is that?" said the princess.

"If only a roc's egg," replied he, "were hung up from the middle of this dome, it would be the wonder of the world." After this the princess could think of nothing but a roc's egg and when Aladdin returned from hunting he found her in a very ill humour. He begged to know what was amiss and she told him that all her pleasure in the hall was spoilt for the want of a roc's egg hanging from the dome.

"If that is all," replied Aladdin, "you shall soon be happy."

He left her and rubbed the lamp and when the genie appeared commanded him to bring a roc's egg. The genie gave such a loud and terrible shriek that the hall shook.

"Wretch!" he cried, "is it not enough that I have done everything for you, but you must command me to bring my master and hang him up in the midst of this dome? You and your wife and your palace deserve to be burnt to ashes, but this request does not come from you, but from the brother of the African magician whom you destroyed. He is now in your palace disguised as the holy woman whom he murdered. He it was who put that wish into your wife's head. Take care of yourself, for he means to kill you." So saying the genie disappeared.

Aladdin went back to the princess, saying his head ached and requesting that the holy Fatima should be fetched to lay her hands on it. But when the magician came near, Aladdin, seizing his dagger, pierced him to the heart.

"What have you done?" cried the princess. "You have killed the holy woman!"

"Not so," replied Aladdin, "but a wicked magician," and told her of how she had been deceived.

After this Aladdin and his wife lived in peace. He succeeded the Sultan when he died and reigned for many years, leaving behind him a long line of kings.

The Sweep
and the Noble Lady

Illustrated by Ella Tjader

During the season of the Meccan pilgrimage, whilst the people were making circuit about the Holy House and the place of compassing was crowded, behold, a man laid hold of the covering of the Ka'aba and cried out from the bottom of his heart, saying, "I beseech thee, O Allah, that she may once again be wroth with her husband and that I may know her!"

A company of the pilgrims heard him and seized him and carried him to the Emir of the pilgrims, after a sufficiency of blows, they said, "O Emir, we found this fellow in the Holy Places, saying thus and thus."

So the Emir commanded to hang him, but he cried, "O Emir, I conjure thee, by the virtue of the Apostle, hear my story and then do with me as thou wilt."

Quoth the Emir, "Tell thy tale forthright."

"Know then, O Emir," quoth the man, "that I am a sweep who works in the sheep slaughterhouses and carries off the blood and the offal to the rubbish heaps outside the gates. And it came to pass as I went along one day with my ass loaded, I saw the people running away and one of them said to me, 'Enter this alley, lest haply they slay thee.'

Quoth I, 'What aileth the people running away?' and one of the eunuchs who were passing said to me, 'This is the harem of one of the notables and her eunuchs drive the people out of her way and beat them all, without respect.'

So I turned aside with the donkey and stood still awaiting the dispersal of the crowd and I saw a number of eunuchs with staves in their hands, followed by nigh thirty women slaves and amongst them a lady as she were a willow wand or a thirsty gazelle, perfect in beauty and grace and amorous languor and all were attending upon her. Now when she came to the mouth of the passage where I stood, she turned right and left and

calling one of the castratos, whispered in his ear and behold, he came up to me and laid hold of me, whilst another eunuch took my ass and made off with it. And when the spectators fled, the first eunuch bound me with a rope and dragged me after him, until I knew not what to do and the people followed us and cried out, saying, 'This is not allowed of Allah! What hath this poor scavenger done that he should be bound with ropes?'

'Have pity on him and let him go, so Allah have pity on you!'

And I the while said in my mind, 'Doubtless the eunuchry seized me because their mistress smelt the stink of the offal and it sickened her. Belike she is with child or ailing, but there is no Majesty and there is no Might save in Allah, the Glorious, the Great!'

So I continued walking on behind them until they stopped at the door of a great house and, entering before me, brought me into a big hall, I know not how I shall describe its magnificence, furnished with the finest furniture. And the women also entered the hall and I bound and held by the eunuch and saying to myself, 'Doubtless they will torture me here until I die and none know of my death.'

However, after a while they carried me into a neat bathroom leading out of the hall and

34

as I sat there, behold, in came three slave girls, who seated themselves round me and said to me, 'Strip off thy rags and tatters.'

So I pulled off my threadbare clothes and one of them fell a-rubbing my legs and feet whilst another scrubbed my head and a third shampooed my body. When they had made an end of washing me, they brought me a parcel of clothes and said to me, 'Put these on,' and I answered, 'By Allah, I know not how!'

So they came up to me and dressed me, laughing together at me the while. After which they brought casting bottles full of rose-water and sprinkled me therewith. Then I went out with them into another saloon, by Allah, I know not how to praise its splendour for the wealth of paintings and furniture therein, and entering it, I saw a person seated on a couch of Indian rattan with ivory feet and before her a number of damsels. When she saw me, she rose to me and called me, so I went up to her and she seated me by her side. Then she bade her slave girls to bring food and they brought all manner of rich meats, such as I had never seen in all my life. I do not even know the names of the dishes, much less their nature. So I ate my fill and when the dishes had been taken away and we had washed our hands, she called for fruits, which came without stay or delay and ordered me to eat of them. And when we had ended eating she bade one of the waiting women to bring the wine furniture. So they set on flagons of divers kinds of wine and burned perfumes in all the censers, while a damsel like the moon rose and served us with wine to the sound of the smitten strings. And I drank and the lady drank, until we were swized with wine and the whole time I doubted not that all this was an illusion of sleep.

Presently, she signed to one of the damsels to spread us a bed in such a place, which being done, she rose and took me by the hand and led me thither and lay down and I lay with her until the morning and as often as I pressed her to my breast I smelt the delicious fragrance of musk and other perfumes that exhaled from her and could not think otherwise but that I was in paradise or in the vain fantasies of a dream.

Now when it was day, she asked me where I lodged and I told her, 'In such a place,' whereupon she gave me leave to depart, handing to me a kerchief worked with gold and silver and containing somewhat tied in it and took leave of me, saying, 'Go to the bath with this.'

I rejoiced and said to myself, 'If there be but five coppers here, it will buy me this day my morning meal.'

Then I left her, as though I were leaving paradise and returned to my poor crib, where I opened the kerchief and found in it fifty miskals of gold. So I buried them in the ground and, buying two farthings' worth of food, seated me at the door and broke my fast. After which I sat pondering my case and continued so doing until the time of afternoon prayer, when suddenly a slave girl accosted me saying, 'My mistress calleth for thee.'

I followed her to the house aforesaid and, after asking permission, she carried me into the lady, before whom I kissed the ground and she commanded me to sit and called for meat and wine as on the previous day. After which I again lay with her all night. On the morrow, she gave me a second kerchief, with other fifty dinars therein and I took it and, going home, buried this also. In such pleasant condition I continued eight days running, going in to her at the hour of afternoon prayer and leaving her at daybreak, but on the eighth night, as I lay with her, behold, one of her slave girls came running in and said to me, 'Arise, go up into yonder closet.'

So I rose and went into the closet, which was over the gate and presently I heard a great clamour and tramp of horse and, looking out of the window which gave on the street in front of the house, I saw a young man as he were the rising moon on the night of fullness come riding up attended by a number of servants and soldiers who were about him on foot. He alighted at the door and entering the saloon, found the lady seated on the couch. So he kissed the ground between her hands, then came up to her and kissed her hands, but she would not speak to him. However, he continued patiently to humble himself and soothe her and speak her fair, until he made his peace with her and they lay together that night.

Now when her husband had made his peace with the young lady, he lay with her that night and next morning the soldiers came for him and he mounted and rode away, whereupon she drew near to me and said, 'Sawest thou yonder man?'

I answered, 'Yes,' and she said, 'He is my husband and I will tell thee what befell me with him. It came to pass one, day that we were sitting, he and I, in the garden within the house and behold, he rose from my side and was absent a long while, until I grew tired of waiting and said to myself, 'Most like, he is in the privy.' So I arose and went to the water closet, but not finding him there, went down to the kitchen, where I saw a slave girl and when I enquired for him, she showed him to me lying with one of the cookmaids. Hereupon I swore a great oath that I assuredly would do adultery with the foulest and filthiest man in Baghdad and the day the eunuch laid hands on thee, I had

been four days going round about the city in quest of one who should answer to this description, but found none fouler nor filthier than thy good self. So I took thee and there passed between us that which Allah foreordained to us and now I am quit of my oath.'

Then she added, 'If, however, my husband return yet a pin to the cookmaid and lie with her, I will restore thee to thy lost place in my favours.'

Now when I heard these words from her lips, what while she pierced my heart with the shafts of her glances, my tears streamed forth until my eyelids were chafed sore with weeping. Then she made them give me another fifty dinars, making in all four hundred gold pieces I had of her, and bade me depart. So I went out from her and came hither, that I might pray Allah to make her husband return to the cookmaid, that haply I might again be admitted to her favours."

When the Emir of the pilgrims heard the man's story, he set him free and said to the bystanders, "Allah upon you, pray for him, for indeed he is excusable."

40

The Tale of
the Three Apples

Illustrated by Katharina Leuzinger

The Caliph Harun al-Rashid summoned his Vizir Ja'afar one night and said to him, "I desire to go down into the city and question the common people concerning the conduct of those charged with its governance and those of whom they complain we will depose from office and those whom they commend we will promote."

So the Caliph went down with Ja'afar and the eunuch Masrur to the town and walked about the streets and markets and as they were threading a narrow alley, they came upon a very old man with a fishing net and crate to carry small fish on his head and in his hands a staff. When the Caliph saw this man, he accosted him and asked, "O Sheikh, what be thine occupation?"

And the poor man answered, "O my lord, I am a fisherman with a family to keep and I have been out between midday and this time and not a thing hath Allah made my portion wherewithal to feed my family. I cannot even pawn myself to buy them a supper and I hate and disgust my life and I hanker after death."

Quoth the Caliph, "Say me, wilt thou return with us to Tigris' bank and cast thy net on my luck and whatsoever turneth up I will buy of thee for one hundred gold pieces?"

The man rejoiced when he heard these words and said, "On my head be it! I will go back with you," and, returning with them riverward, made a cast and waited a while. Then he hauled in the rope and dragged the net ashore and there appeared in it a chest, padlocked and heavy. The Caliph examined it and lifted it, finding it weighty, so he gave the fisherman two hundred dinars and sent him about his business whilst Masrur, aided by the Caliph, carried the chest to the palace and set it down and lighted the candles. Ja'afar and Masrur then broke it open and found therein a basket of palm leaves corded with red worsted. This they cut open and saw within it a piece of carpet, which they lifted out and under it was a woman's mantilla folded in four, which they pulled

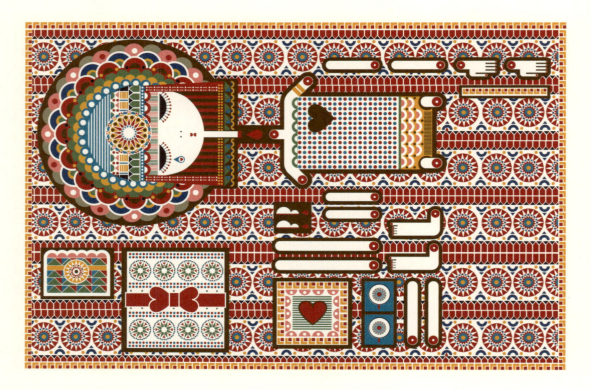

out and at the bottom of the chest they came upon a young lady, fair as a silver ingot, slain and cut into nineteen pieces. When the Caliph looked upon her he cried, "Alas!" and tears ran down his cheeks and turning to Ja'afar, he said, "O Ja'afar, shall people be murdered in our reign and be cast into the river to be a burden and a responsibility for us on the Day of Doom? By Allah, we must avenge this woman on her murderer and he shall be made die the worst of deaths!"

And presently he added, "Now, as surely as we are descended from the Sons of Abbas, if thou bring us not him who slew her, that we do her justice on him, I will hang thee at the gate of my palace, thee and forty of thy kith and kin by thy side." And the Caliph was wroth with exceeding rage.

Quoth Ja'afar, "Grant me three days' delay," and quoth the Caliph, "We grant thee this."

So Ja'afar went out from before him and returned to his own house, full of sorrow and saying to himself, "How shall I find him who murdered this damsel, that I may bring him before the Caliph? If I bring other than the murderer, it will be laid to my charge by the Lord. In very sooth I know not what to do." He kept to his house for three days and on the fourth day the Caliph sent one of the chamberlains for him and as he came into the presence, asked him, "Where is the murderer of the damsel?"

To which answered Ja'afar, "O Commander of the Faithful, am I inspector of murdered people that I should ken who killed her?"

The Caliph was furious at his answer and bade to hang him before the palace gate and commanded that a crier cry through the streets of Baghdad, "Whoso would see the hanging of Ja'afar, the Barmaki, Vizir of the Caliph, with forty of the Barmecides, his cousins and kinsmen, before the palace gate, let him come and let him look!"

The people flocked out from all the quarters of the city to witness the execution of Ja'afar and his kinsmen, not knowing the cause. Then they set up the gallows and made Ja'afar and the others stand underneath in readiness for execution, but whilst every eye was looking for the Caliph's signal and the crowd wept for Ja'afar and his cousins of the Barmecides, lo and behold, a young man fair of face and neat of dress and of favour like the moon raining fight, with eyes black and bright and brow flower-white and cheeks red as rose and young down where the beard grows and a mole like a grain of ambergris, pushed his way through the people until he stood immediately before the Vizir and said to him, "Safety to thee from this strait, O Prince of the Emirs and Asylum of the Poor! I am the man who slew the woman ye found in the chest, so hang me for her and do her justice on me!"

When Ja'afar heard the youth's confession he rejoiced at his own deliverance, but grieved and sorrowed for the fair youth. And whilst they were yet talking, behold, another man well stricken in years pressed forward through the people and thrust his way amid the populace until he came to Ja'afar and the youth, whom he saluted, saying, "Ho, thou the Vizir! Believe not the words of this youth. Of a surety none murdered the damsel but I. Take her wreak on me this moment, for if thou do not thus, I will require it of thee before Almighty Allah."

Then quoth the young man, "O Vizir, this is an old man in his dotage who wotteth not whatso he saith ever and I am he who murdered her, so do thou avenge her on me!"

Quoth the old man, "O my son, thou art young and desirest the joys of the world and I am old and weary and surfeited with the world. I will offer my life as a ransom for thee and for the Vizir and his cousins. No one murdered the damsel but I, so Allah upon thee, make haste to hang me, for no life is left in me now that hers is gone."

The Vizir marvelled much at all this strangeness and taking the young man and the old man, carried them before the Caliph, where, after kissing the ground seven times between his hands, he said, "O Commander of the Faithful, I bring thee the murderer of the damsel!" "Where is he?" asked the Caliph and Ja'afar answered, "This young man saith, 'I am the murderer,' and this old man, giving him the lie, saith, 'I am the murderer,' and behold, here are the twain standing before thee."

The Caliph looked at the old man and the young man and asked, "Which of you killed the girl?"

The young man replied, "No one slew her save I," and the old man answered, "Indeed none killed her but myself."

Then said the Caliph to Ja'afar, "Take the twain and hang them both."

But Ja'afar rejoined, "Since one of them was the murderer, to hang the other were mere injustice."

"By Him who raised the firmament and dispread the earth like a carpet," cried the youth, "I am he who slew the damsel," and he went on to describe the manner of her murder and the basket, the mantilla and the bit of carpet, in fact, all that the Caliph had found upon her.

So the Caliph was certified that the young man was the murderer, whereat he wondered and asked him, "What was the cause of thy wrongfully doing this damsel to die and what made thee confess the murder without the bastinado and what brought thee here to yield up thy life and what made thee say 'Do her wreak upon me'?"

The youth answered, "Know, O Commander of the Faithful, that this woman was my wife and the mother of my children, also my first cousin and the daughter of my paternal uncle, this old man, who is my father's own brother. When I married her she was a maid and Allah blessed me with three male children by her. She loved me and served me and I saw no evil in her, for I also loved her with fondest love. Now on the first day of this month she fell ill with grievous sickness and I fetched in physicians to her, but recovery came to her little by little and when I wished her to go to the hammam bath, she said, 'There is something I long for before I go to the bath and I long for it with an exceeding longing.'

'To hear is to comply,' said I. 'And what is it?'

Quoth she, 'I have a queasy craving for an apple, to smell it and bite a bit of it.'

I replied, 'Hadst thou a thousand longings, I would try to satisfy them!'

So I went on the instant into the city and sought for apples, but could find none, yet

45

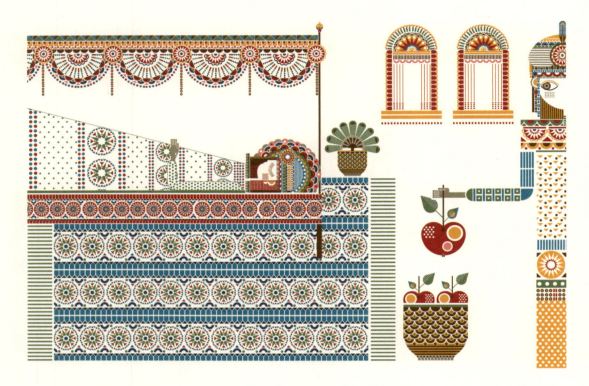

had they cost a gold piece each, would I have bought them. I was vexed at this and went home and said, 'O daughter of my uncle, by Allah I can find none!'

She was distressed, being yet very weakly and her weakness increased greatly on her that night and I felt anxious and alarmed on her account. As soon as morning dawned I went out again and made the round of the gardens, one by one, but found no apples anywhere. At last there met me an old gardener, of whom I asked about them and he answered, 'O my son, this fruit is a rarity with us and is not now to be found save in the garden of the Commander of the Faithful at Bassorah, where the gardener keepeth it for the Caliph's eating.'

I returned to my house troubled by my ill success and my love for my wife and my affection moved me to undertake the journey. So I made ready and set out and travelled fifteen days and nights, going and coming and brought her three apples, which I bought from the gardener for three dinars.

But when I went in to my wife and set them before her, she took no pleasure in them and let them lie by her side, for her weakness and fever had increased on her and her malady lasted without abating ten days, after which she began to recover health. So I left my house and betaking me to my shop, sat there buying and selling. At about mid-day, behold, a great ugly slave, long as a lance and broad as a bench, passed by my shop holding in hand one of the three apples, wherewith he was playing, quoth I, 'O my good slave, tell me whence thou tookest that apple, that I may get the like of it?'

He laughed and answered, 'I got it from my mistress, for I had been absent and on my return I found her lying ill with three apples by her side and she said to me, 'My horned wit-tol of a husband made a journey for them to Bassorah and bought them for three dinars.' 'So I ate and drank with her and took this one from her.'

When I heard such words from the slave, O Commander of the Faithful, the world grew black before my face and I arose and locked up my shop and went home beside myself for excess of rage. I looked for the apples and finding only two of the three, asked my wife, 'O my cousin, where is the third apple?'

And raising her head languidly, she answered, 'I wot not, O son of my uncle, where 'tis gone!'

This convinced me that the slave had spoken the truth, so I took a knife and coming behind her, got upon her breast without a word said and cut her throat. Then I hewed off her head and her limbs in pieces and, wrapping her in her mantilla and a rag of carpet, hurriedly sewed up the whole, which I set in a chest and, locking it tight, loaded it on my he-mule and threw it into the Tigris with my own hands.

So Allah upon thee, O Commander of the Faithful, make haste to hang me, as I fear lest she appeal for vengeance on Resurrection Day. For when I had thrown her into the river and one knew aught of it, as I went back home I found my eldest son crying and yet he knew naught of what I had done with his mother. I asked him, 'What hath made thee weep, my boy?' and he answered, 'I took one of the three apples which were by my mammy and went down into the lane to play with my brethren when, behold, a big long slave snatched it from my hand and said, 'Whence hadst thou this?'

Quoth I, 'My father travelled far for it and brought it from Bassorah for my mother, who was ill and two other apples for which he paid three ducats.'

'He took no heed of my words and I asked for the apple a second and a third time, but he cuffed me and kicked me and went off with it. I was afraid lest my mother should scold me on account of the apple, so for fear of her I went with my brother outside the city and stayed there until evening closed in upon us and indeed I am in fear of her. And now, by Allah, O my father, say nothing to her of this or it may add to her ailment!'

When I heard what my child said, I knew that the slave was he who had foully slandered my wife, the daughter of my uncle and was certified that I had slain her wrongfully. So I wept with exceeding weeping and presently this old man, my paternal uncle and her father, came in and I told him what had happened and he sat down by my side and wept and we ceased not weeping until midnight. We have kept up mourning for her these last five days and we lamented her in the deepest sorrow for that she was unjustly done to die. This came from the gratuitous lying of the slave and this was the manner of my killing her. So I conjure thee, by the honour of thine ancestors, make haste to kill me and do her justice upon me, as there is no living for me after her!"

The Caliph marvelled at his words and said, "By Allah, the young man is excusable. I will hang none but the accursed slave and I will do a deed which shall comfort the ill-at-ease and suffering and which shall please the All-glorious King."

Then he turned to Ja'afar and said to him, "Bring before me this accursed slave who was the sole cause of this calamity and if thou bring him not before me within three days, thou shalt be slain in his stead."

So Ja'afar fared forth weeping and saying, "Two deaths have already beset me, nor shall the crock come off safe from every shock. In this matter craft and cunning are of no avail, but He who preserved my life the first time can preserve it a second time. By Allah, I will not leave my house during the three days of life which remain to me."

So he kept to his house for three days and on the fourth day he summoned the kazis and legal witnesses and made his last will and testament and took leave of his children weeping. Presently in came a messenger from the Caliph and said to him, "The Commander of the Faithful is in the most violent rage that can be and he sendeth to seek thee and he sweareth that the day shall certainly not pass without thy being hanged unless the slave be forth-coming."

When Ja'afar heard this he wept and his children and slaves and all who were in the house wept with him. After he had bidden adieu to everybody except his youngest daughter, he proceeded to farewell her, for he loved this wee one, who was a beautiful child, more than all his other children. And he pressed her to his breast and kissed her and wept bitterly at parting from her, when he felt something round inside the bosom of her dress and asked her, "O my little maid, what is in the bosom pocket?"

"O my father," she replied, "it is an apple with the name of our Lord the Caliph written

49

50

upon it. Rayhan our slave brought it to me four days ago and would not let me have it until I gave him two dinars for it."

When Ja'afar heard speak of the slave and the apple, he was glad and put his hand into his child's pocket and drew out the apple and knew it and rejoiced, saying, "O ready Dispeller of trouble!"

Then he bade them to bring the slave and said to him, "Fie upon thee, Rayhan! Whence haddest thou this apple?"

"By Allah, O my master," he replied, "though He may get a man off once, yet may truth get him off and well off, again and again. I did not steal this apple from thy palace nor from the gardens of the Commander of the Faithful. The fact is that five days ago, as I was walking along one of the alleys of this city, I saw some little ones at play and this apple in the hand of one of them. So I snatched it from him and beat him and he cried and said, 'O youth, this apple is my mother's and she is ill. She told my father how she longed for an apple, so he travelled to Bassorah and bought her three apples for three gold pieces and I took one of them to play withal.' He wept again, but I paid no heed to what he said and carried it off and brought it here and my little lady bought it of me for two dinars of gold. And this is the whole story."

When Ja'afar heard his words he marvelled that the murder of the damsel and all this misery should have been caused by his slave. He grieved for the relation of the slave to himself while rejoicing over his own deliverance and he repeated these lines, "If ill betide thee through thy slave, make him forthright thy sacrifice. A many serviles thou shalt find, but life comes once and never twice."

Then he took the slave's hand and, leading him to the Caliph, related the story from first to last and the Caliph marvelled with extreme astonishment and laughed until he fell on his back and ordered that the story be recorded and be made public amongst the people. But Ja'afar said, "Marvel not, O Commander of the Faithful, at this adventure, for it is not more wondrous than the history of the Vizir Nur al-Din Ali of Egypt and his brother Shams al-Din Mohammed."

Quoth the Caliph, "Out with it, but what can be stranger than this story?"

And Ja'afar answered, "O Commander of the Faithful, I will not tell it thee save on condition that thou pardon my slave."

And the Caliph rejoined, "If it be indeed more wondrous than that of the three apples, I grant thee his blood and if not I will surely slay thy slave."

52

The Man who stole
the Dish of Gold
wherein the Dog ate

Illustrated by Jens Harder

A long time ago there was a man who had accumulated debts, and his case was straitened upon him so that he left his people and family and went forth in distraction, and
he ceased not wandering on at random until he came after a time to a city tall of walls
and firm of foundations. He entered it in a state of despondency and despair, harried
by hunger and worn with the weariness of his way. As he passed through one of the
main streets, he saw a company of the great going along, so he followed them until they
reached a house like to a royal palace. He entered with them, and they stayed not faring
forward until they came in presence of a person seated at the upper end of a saloon, a
man of the most dignified and majestic aspect, surrounded by pages and eunuchs, as
he were of the sons of the Vizirs. When he saw the visitors, he rose to greet them and
received them with honour, but the poor man aforesaid was confounded at his own
boldness when beholding the goodliness of the place and the crowd of servants and
attendants, so drawing back in perplexity and fear for his life, sat down apart in a place
afar off, where none should see him.

Now it chanced that whilst he was sitting, behold, in came a man with four sporting dogs,
whereon were various kinds of raw silk and brocade and wearing round their necks collars of gold with chains of silver, and tied up each dog in a place set privy for him. After
which he went out and presently returned with four dishes of gold, full of rich meats,
which he set severally before the dogs, one for each. Then he went away and left them,
whilst the poor man began to eye the food for stress of hunger and longed to go up to
one of the dogs and eat with him. But fear of them withheld him. Presently, one of the
dogs looked at him and Allah Almighty inspired the dog with knowledge of his case, so

he drew back from the platter and signed to the man, who came and ate until he was filled. Then he would have withdrawn, but the dog again signed to him to take for himself the dish and what food was left in it, and pushed it toward him with his forepaw. So the man took the dish and leaving the house, went his way, and none followed him.

Then he journeyed to another city, where he sold the dish and buying with the price a stock in trade, returned to his own town. There he sold his goods and paid his debts and he throve and became affluent and rose to perfect prosperity. He abode in his own land, but after some years had passed he said to himself, "Needs must I repair to the city of the owner of the dish and carry him a fit and handsome present and pay him the money value of that which his dog bestowed upon me."

So he took the price of the dish and a suitable gift, and setting out, journeyed day and night until he came to that city. He entered it and sought the place where the man lived, but he found there naught save ruins mouldering in row and croak of crow, and house and home desolate and all conditions in changed state.

Now when the man saw these mouldering ruins and witnessed what the hand of time had manifestly done with the place, leaving but traces of the substantial things that once had been, a little reflection made it needless for him to inquire of the case, so he turned away. Presently, seeing a wretched man, in a plight which made him shudder and feel goose skin, and which would have moved the very rock to ruth, he said to him, "Ho, thou! What have time and fortune done with the lord of this place? Where are his lovely faces, his shining full moons and splendid stars? And what is the cause of the ruin that is come upon his abode so that nothing save the walls thereof remain?"

Quoth the other, "He is the miserable thou seest mourning that which hath left him naked. But knowest thou not the words of the Apostle, whom Allah bless and keep, wherein is a lesson to him who will learn by it and a warning to whoso will be warned thereby and guided in the right way, 'Verily it is the way of Allah Almighty to raise up nothing of this world, except He cast it down again'. If thou question of the cause of this accident, indeed it is no wonder, considering the chances and changes of fortune. I was the lord of this place and I built it and founded it and owned it, and I was the proud possessor of its full moons lucent and its circumstance resplendent and its damsels radiant and its garniture magnificent, but time turned and did away from me wealth and servants and took from me what it had lent, not given, and brought upon me calamities which it held in store hidden. But there must be some reason for this thy question, so tell it me and leave wondering."

Thereupon the man who had waxed wealthy, being sore concerned, told him the whole story, and added, "I have brought thee a present, such as souls desire, and the price of thy dish of gold which I took; for it was the cause of my affluence after poverty, and of the replenishment of my dwelling place after desolation, and of the dispersion of my trouble and straitness."

But the man shook his head and weeping and groaning and complaining of his lot, answered, "Ho, thou! Methinks thou art mad, for this is not the way of a man of sense. How should a dog of mine make generous gift to thee of a dish of gold and I meanly take back the price of what a dog gave? This were indeed a strange thing! Were I in extremist unease and misery, by Allah, I would not accept of thee aught, no, not the worth of a nail paring! So return whence thou camest in health and safety."

Whereupon the merchant kissed his feet and taking leave of him, returned whence he came.

Sindbad the Seaman

Illustrated by Luise Vormittag & Nicola Carter

There lived in the city of Baghdad during the reign of the Commander of the Faithful, Harun al-Rashid, a man named Sindbad the Hammal, one in poor case who bore burdens on his head for hire. It happened to him one day of great heat that whilst he was carrying a heavy load, he became exceedingly weary and sweated profusely, the heat and the weight alike oppressing him.

Presently, as he was passing the gate of a merchant's house before which the ground was swept and watered and where the air was temperate, he sighted a broad bench beside the door, so he set his load thereon, to take rest and smell the air. He sat down on the edge of the bench and at once heard from within the melodious sound of lutes and other stringed instruments and mirth-exciting voices singing and reciting, together with the song of birds warbling and glorifying Almighty Allah in various tunes and tongues turtles, mocking birds, merles, nightingales, cushats and stone curlews - whereat he marvelled in himself and was moved to mighty joy and solace.

Then he went up to the gate and saw within a great flower garden wherein were pages and slaves and such a train of servants and attendants and so forth as is found only with Kings and Sultans. And his nostrils were greeted with the savoury odours of a manner of meats rich and delicate and delicious and generous wines.

So he raised his eyes heavenward and said, "Glory to Thee, O Lord, O Creator and Provider, Who providest whomso Thou wilt without count or stint! O mine Holy One, I cry Thee pardon for my sins and turn to Thee repenting of all offences! O Lord,, there is no gainsaying Thee in thine ordinance and Thy dominion, neither wilt Thou be questioned of that Thou dost, for Thou indeed over all things art Allmighty! Extolled be Thy prefection: whom Thou wilt Thou makest poor and whom Thou wilt Thou makest rich! Whom thou wilt Thou exaltest and whom Thou wilt Thou abasest and there is no god but Thou! How mighty is Thy majesty and how enduring Thy dominion and how excellent

Thy government! Verily, Thou favourest whom Thou wilt of Thy servants, whereby the owner of this place abideth in all joyance of life and delighteth himself with pleasant scents and delicious meats and exquisite wines of all kinds. For indeed Thou appointest unto Thy creatures that which Thou wilt and that which Thou hast foreordained unto them; wherefore are some weary and others are at rest and some enjoy fair fortune and affluence, whilst others suffer the extreme of travail amd misery, even as I do."

And he fell to reciting, how many by my labours, that evermore endure, all goods of life enjoy and in cooly shade recline? Each morn that dawns I wake in travail and in woe, and strange is my condition and my burden causes me pine. Many others are in luck and from miseries are free and fortune never load them with loads the like of mine. They live their happy days in all solace and delight, eat, drink and dwell in honour amid the noble and the dignified. All living things were made of a little drop of sperm, thine origin is mine and my provenance is thine, yet the difference and distance 'twixt the twain of us are far as the difference of savour 'twixt vinegar and wine. But at Thee, O God all-wise! I venture not to rail, whose ordinance is just and whose justice cannot fail."

When Sindbad the Porter had made an end of reciting his verses, he bore up his burden and was about to fare on when there came forth to him from the gate a little foot page, fair of face and shapely of shape and dainty of dress, who caught him by the hand saying, "Come in and speak with my lord, for he calleth for thee."

The porter would have excused himself to the page, but the lad would take no refusal, so he left his load with the doorkeeper in the vestibule and followed the boy into the house, which he found to be a goodly mansion, radiant and full of majesty, until he brought him to a grand sitting room wherein he saw a company of nobles and great lords seated at tables garnished with all manner of flowers and sweet-scented herbs, besides great plenty of dainty viands and fruits dried and fresh and confections and wines of the choicest vintages.

There were also instruments of music and mirth and lovely slave girls playing and singing. All the company was ranged according to rank and in the highest place sat a man of worshipful and noble aspect whose beard sides hoariness had stricken and he was stately of stature and fair of favour, agreeable of aspect and full of gravity and dignity and majesty.

So Sindbad the Porter was confounded at that which he beheld and said in himself, "By Allah, this must be either a piece of Paradise or some king's palace!" Then he saluted

the company with much respect, praying for their prosperity and kissing the ground before them, stood with his head bowed down in humble attitude.

The master of the house bade him to draw near and be seated and bespoke him kindly, bidding him welcome. Then he set before him various kinds of viands, rich and delicate and delicious and the porter, after saying his Bismillah, fell to and ate his fill, after which he exclaimed, "Praised be Allah, whatso be our case!" and, washing his hands, returned thanks to the company for his entertainment.

Quoth the host, "Thou art welcome and thy day is a blessed. But what is thy name and calling?"

Quoth the other, "O my lord, my name is Sindbad the Hammal and I carry people's goods on my head for hire."

The housemaster smiled and rejoined, "Know, O porter that thy name is even as mine, for I am Sindbad the Seaman. And now, O porter, I would have thee let me hear the couplets thou recitedst at the gate anon."

The porter was abashed and replied, "Allah upon thee! Excuse me, for toil and travail and lack of luck when the hand is empty teach a man ill manners and boorish ways."

60

Said the host, "Be not ashamed. Thou art become my brother. But repeat to me the verses, for they pleased me whenas I heard thee recite them at the gate."

Hereupon the porter repeated the couplets and they delighted the merchant, who said to him, "Know, O Hammal, that my story is a wonderful one and thou shalt hear all that befell me and all I underwent ere I rose to this state of prosperity and became the lord of this place wherein thou seest me. For I came not to this high estate save after travail sore and perils galore and how much toil and trouble have I not suffered in days of yore! I have made seven voyages, by each of which hangeth a marvellous tale, such as confoundeth the reason and all this came to pass by doom of fortune and fate. For from what destiny doth write there is neither refuge nor flight. Know, then, good my lords," continued he, "that I am about to relate the First Voyage of Sindbad the Seaman."

The First Voyage of Sindbad the Seaman

Illustrated by Simone Legno

My father was a merchant, one of the notables of my native place, a moneyed man and ample of means, who died whilst I was yet a child, leaving me much wealth in money and lands and farmhouses. When I grew up, I laid hands on the whole and ate of the best and drank freely and wore rich clothes and lived lavishly, companioning and consorting with youths of my own age and considering that this course of life would continue forever and know no change. Thus I did for a long time, but at last I awoke from my heedlessness and, returning to my senses, I found my wealth had become unwealth and my condition ill-conditioned and all I once owned had left my hand. And recovering my reason, I was stricken with dismay and confusion and bethought me of a saying of our lord Solomon, son of David which I had heard aforetime from my father, "Things are better than other three. The day of death is better than the day of birth, a live dog is better than a dead lion and the grave is better than want."

Then I got together my remains of estates and property and sold all, even my clothes, for three thousand dirhams, with which I resolved to travel to foreign parts, remembering the saying of the poet, "By means of toil man shall scale the height, who to fame aspires mustn't sleep of night. Who seeketh pearl in the deep must dive, winning weal and wealth by his main and might. And who seeketh fame without toil and strife, impossible seeketh and wasteth life."

So, taking heart, I bought me goods, merchandise and all needed for a voyage and impatient to be at sea, I embarked, with a company of merchants, on board a ship bound for Bassorah. There we again embarked and sailed many days and nights and we passed from isle to isle and sea to sea and shore to shore, buying and selling and bartering everywhere the ship touched and continued our course until we came to an island as it were a garth of the gardens of Paradise. Here the captain cast anchor and, making fast to the shore, put out the landing planks. So all on board landed and made furnaces and lighting fires therein, busied themselves in various ways, some cooking and some washing, whilst some walked about the island for solace and the crew fell to eating and drinking and playing and sporting. I was one of the walkers, but as we were thus engaged, behold the master, who was standing on the gunwale, cried out to us at the top of his voice, saying, "Ho there! Passengers, run for your lives and hasten back to the ship and leave your gear and save yourselves from destruction, Allah preserve you! For this island whereon ye stand is no true island, but a great fish stationary a-middlemost of the sea, whereon the sand hath settled and trees have sprung up of old time, so that it was become like an island. But when ye lighted fires on it, it felt the heat and moved and in a moment it will sink with you into the sea and ye will all be drowned. So leave your gear and seek your safety ere ye die!"

All who heard him left gear and goods, clothes washed and unwashed, fire pots and brass cooking pots and fled back to the ship for their lives, some reached it while others, amongst whom was I, did not, for suddenly the island shook and sank into the abysses of the deep, with all that were thereon and the dashing sea surged over it with clashing waves. I sank with the others down, down into the deep, but Almighty Allah preserved me from drowning and threw in my way a great wooden tub of those that had served the ship's company for bathing. I gripped it for the sweetness of life and, bestriding it like one riding, paddled with my feet like oars, whilst the waves tossed me as in sport right and left.

Meanwhile the captain made sail and departed with those who had reached the ship, regardless of the drowning and the drowned. And I ceased not following the vessel with my eyes until she was hid from sight and I made sure of death. Darkness closed in upon me while in this plight, and the winds and waves bore me on all that night and the next day until the tub brought to with me under the lee of a lofty island with trees overhanging the tide. I caught hold of a branch and by its aid clambered up onto the land, after coming nigh upon death. But when I reached the shore, I found my legs cramped and numbed and my feet bore traces of the nibbling of fish upon their soles, withal I had felt nothing for excess of anguish and fatigue. I threw myself down on the island ground like a dead man and drowned in desolation, swooned away, nor did I return to my senses until next morning, when the sun rose and revived me. But I found my feet swollen, so made shift to move by shuffling on my breech and crawling on my knees,

for in that island were found a store of fruits and springs of sweet water. I ate of the fruits, which strengthened me. And thus I abode days and nights until my life seemed to return and my spirits began to revive and I was better able to move about. So, after due consideration, I fell to exploring the island and diverting myself with gazing upon all things that Allah Almighty had created there and rested under the trees, from one of which I cut me a staff to lean upon.

One day as I walked along the marge I caught sight of some object in the distance and thought it a wild beast or one of the monster creatures of the sea, but as I drew near it, looking hard the while, I saw that it was a noble mare, tethered on the beach. Presently I went up to her, but she cried out against me with a great cry, so that I trembled for fear and turned to go away, when there came forth a man from under the earth and followed me, crying out and saying, "Who and whence art thou and what caused thee to come hither?"

"O my lord," answered I, "I am in very sooth a waif, a stranger and was left to drown with sundry others by the ship we voyaged in. But Allah graciously sent me a wooden tub, so I saved myself thereon and it floated with me, until the waves cast me up on this island."

When he heard this, he took my hand and saying, "Come with me," carried me into a great sardab, or underground chamber, which was as spacious as a saloon. He made me sit down at its upper end, then he brought me somewhat of food and, being a-hungered, I ate until I was satisfied and refreshed. And after he had put me at ease, he questioned me of myself and I told him all that had befallen me from first to last.

And as he wondered at my adventure, I said, "By Allah, O my lord, excuse me, I have told thee the truth of my case and the accident which betided me and now I desire that thou tell me who thou art and why thou abidest here under the earth and why thou hast tethered yonder mare on the brink of the sea."

Answered he, "Know that I am one of the several who are stationed in different parts of this island and we are the grooms of King Mihrjan and under our hand are all his horses. Every month about new-moon tide we bring hither our best mares which have never been covered and picket them on the seashore and hide ourselves in this place under the ground, so that none may espy us. Presently the stallions of the sea scent the mares and come up out of the water and, seeing no one, leap the mares and do their will of them. When they have covered them, they try to drag them away with them, but cannot, by reason of the leg ropes. So they cry out at them and butt at them and kick them, which we hearing, know that the stallions have dismounted, so we run out and shout at them, whereupon they are startled and return in fear to the sea. Then the mares conceive by them and bear colts and fillies worth a mint of money, nor is their like to be found on earth's face. This is the time of the coming forth of the sea stallions and Inshallah! I will bear thee to King Mihrjan and show thee our country. And know that hadst thou not happened on us, thou hadst perished miserably and none would have known of thee. But I will be the means of the saving of thy life and of thy return to thine own land."

I called down blessings on him and thanked him for his kindness and courtesy. And while we were yet talking, behold, the stallion came up out of the sea and, giving a great cry, sprang upon the mare and covered her. When he had done his will of her, he dismounted and would have carried her away with him, but could not by reason of the tether. She kicked and cried out at him, whereupon the groom took a sword and target and ran out of the underground saloon, smitting the buckler with the blade and calling to his company, who came up shouting and brandishing spears. And the stallion took fright at them and plunging into the sea like a buffalo, disappeared under the waves.

After this we sat awhile until the rest of the grooms came up, each leading a mare and seeing me with their fellow syce, questioned me of my case and I repeated my story to them. Thereupon they drew near me and spreading the table, ate and invited me to eat. So I ate with them, after which they took horse and mounting me on one of the mares, set out with me and fared on without ceasing until we came to the capital city of King Mihrjan and going in to him, acquainted him with my story.

Then he sent for me and when they set me before him and salaams had been exchanged, he gave me a cordial welcome and wishing me long life, bade me to tell him my tale. So I related to him all that I had seen and all that had befallen me from first to last, whereat he marvelled and said to me, "By Allah, O my son, thou hast indeed been miraculously preserved! Were not the term of thy life a long one, thou hadst not escaped from these straits. But praised be Allah for safety!"

Then he spoke cheerily to me and entreated me with kindness and consideration. Moreover, he made me his agent for the port and registrar of all ships that entered the harbour. I attended him regularly to receive his commandments and he favoured me and did me all manner of kindness and invested me with costly and splendid robes. Indeed,

I was high in credit with him as an intercessor for the people and an intermediary between them and him when they wanted aught of him. I abode thus a great while and as often as I passed through the city to the port I questioned the merchants and travellers and sailors of the city of Baghdad, so haply I might hear of an occasion to return to my native land, but could find none who knew it or knew any who resorted thither.

At this I was chagrined, for I was weary of long strangerhood and my disappointment endured for a time until one day, going in to King Mihrjan, I found with him a company of Indians. I saluted them and they returned my salaam and politely welcomed me and asked me of my country. When they asked me of my country, I questioned them of theirs and they told me that they were of various castes, some being called Shakiriyah, who are the noblest of their casts and neither oppress nor offer violence to any and others Brahmans, a folk who abstain from wine but live in delight and solace and merriment and own camels and horses and cattle. Moreover, they told me that the people of India are divided into two and seventy castes and I marvelled at this with exceeding marvel. Amongst other things that I saw in King Mihrijan's dominions was an island called Kasil, wherein all night is heard the beating of drums and tabrets, but we were told by the neighbouring islanders and by travellers that the inhabitants are people of diligence and judgment. In this sea I also saw a fish two hundred cubits long which the fishermen fear, so they strike together pieces of wood and put it to flight. I also saw another fish with a head like that of an owl, besides many other wonders and rarities, which it would be tedious to recount.

I occupied myself thus in visiting the islands until one day as I stood in the port with a staff in my hand, according to my custom, behold, a great ship, wherein were many merchants, came sailing for the harbour. When it reached the small inner port where ships anchor under the city, the master furled his sails and making fast to the shore, put out the landing planks, whereupon the crew fell to breaking bulk and landing cargo whilst I stood by, taking written note of them. They were long in bringing the goods ashore, so I asked the master, "Is there aught left in thy ship?" and he answered, "O my lord, there are divers bales of merchandise in the hold, whose owner was drowned from amongst us at one of the islands on our course; so his goods remained in our charge by way of trust and we purpose to sell them and note their price, so that we may convey it to his people in the city of Baghdad, the Home of Peace."

"What was the merchant's name?" quoth I and quoth he, "Sindbad the Seaman," whereupon I straitly considered him and knowing him, cried out to him with a great cry, saying, "O Captain, I am that Sindbad the Seaman who travelled with other merchants and when the fish heaved and thou calledst to us, some saved themselves and others sank, I being one of them. But Allah Almighty threw in my way a great tub of wood, of those the crew had used to wash withal and the winds and waves carried me to this island, where by Allah's grace I fell in with King Mihrjan's grooms and they brought me hither to the King their master."

When I told him my story, he entreated me with favour and made me his harbour-master and I have prospered in his service and found acceptance with him. "These bales therefore are mine, the goods which God hath given me."

The other exclaimed, "There is no Majesty and there is no Might save in Allah, the Glorious, the Great! Verily, there is neither conscience nor good faith left among men!'

Said I, "O Rais, what mean these words, seeing that I have told thee my case?"

And he answered, "Because thou heardest me say that I had with me goods whose owner was drowned, thou thinkest to take them without right. But this is forbidden by law to thee, for we saw him drown before our eyes, together with many other passengers, nor was one of them saved. So how canst thou pretend that thou art the owner of the goods?"

"O Captain," said I, "listen to my story and give heed to my words and my truth will be manifest to thee, for lying and leasing are the letter marks of the hypocrites."

Then I recounted to him all that had befallen me since I sailed from Baghdad with him to the time when we came to the fish island where we were nearly drowned and I reminded him of certain matters which had passed between us. Whereupon both he and the merchants were certified of the truth of my story and recognised me and gave me joy of my deliverance, saying, "By Allah, we thought not that thou hadst escaped drowning! But the Lord hath granted thee new life."

Then they delivered my bales to me and I found my name written thereon, nor was aught thereof lacking. So I opened them and making up a present for King Mihrjan of the finest and costliest of the contents, caused the sailors carry it up to the palace, where I went in to the King and laid my present at his feet, acquainting him with what had happened, especially concerning the ship and my goods, whereat he wondered with exceeding wonder and the truth of that I had told him was made manifest to him.

His affection for me redoubled after that and he showed me exceeding honour and bestowed on me a great present in return for mine. Then I sold my bales and what other matters I owned, making a great profit on them and bought me other goods and gear of the growth and fashion of the island city. When the merchants were about to start on their homeward voyage, I embarked on board the ship all that I possessed and going in to the King, thanked him for all his favours and friendship and craved his leave to return to my own land and friends. He farewelled me and bestowed on me great store of the country stuffs and produce and I took leave of him and embarked. Then we set sail and fared on nights and days, by the permission of Allah Almighty, and fortune served us and fate favoured us, so that we arrived in safety at Bassorah city, where I landed rejoiced at my safe return to my natal soil. After a short stay, I set out for Baghdad, the House of Peace, with store of goods and commodities of great price.

Reaching the city in due time, I went straight to my own quarter and entered my house, where all my friends and kinsfolk came to greet me. Then I bought me eunuchs and concubines, servants and slaves, until I had a large establishment and I bought me houses and lands and gardens, until I was richer and in better case than before and

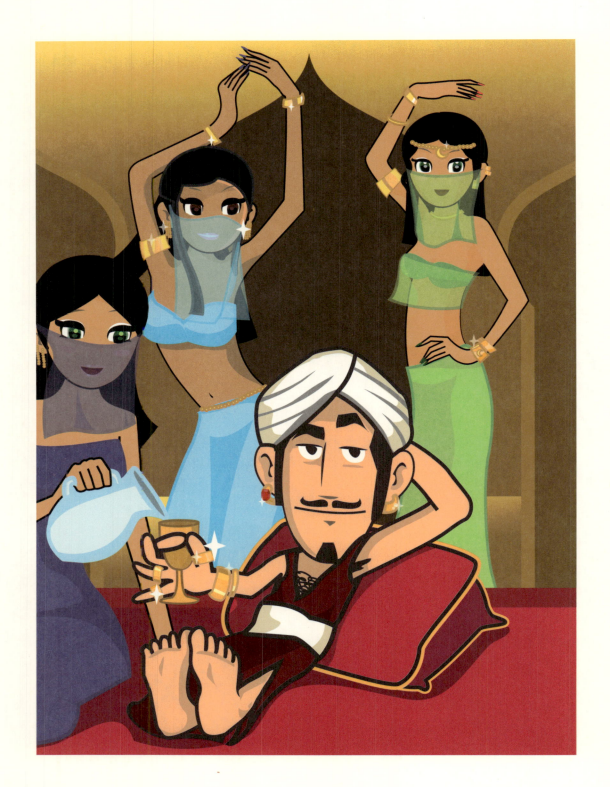

returned to enjoy the society of my friends and familiars more assiduously than ever, forgetting all I had suffered of fatigue and hardship and strangerhood and every peril of travel. And I applied myself to all manner of joys and solaces and delights, eating the daintiest viands and drinking the most delicious wines and my wealth allowed this state of things to endure. This, then, is the story of my first voyage and tomorrow, Inshallah! I will tell you the tale of the second of my seven voyages.

Then Sindbad the Seaman made Sindbad the Landsman sup with him and bade to give him a hundred gold pieces, saying, "Thou hast cheered us with thy company this day." The porter thanked him and, taking the gift, went his way, pondering that which he had heard and marvelling mightily at what things betide mankind. He passed the night in his own place and with early morning repaired to the abode of Sindbad the Seaman, who received him with honour and seated him by his side. As soon as the rest of the company was assembled, he set meat and drink before them and when they had well eaten and drunken and were merry and in cheerful case, he took up his discourse and recounted to them in these words the narrative of the Second Voyage of Sindbad the Seaman.

The Second Voyage of Sindbad the Seaman

Illustrated by Julia Pfaller

Know, O my brother, that I was living a most comfortable and enjoyable life, in all solace and delight, as I told you yesterday, until one day my mind became possessed with the thought of travelling about the world of men and seeing their cities and islands and a longing seized me to traffic and to make money by trade. Upon this resolve I took a great store of cash and buying goods and gear fit for travel, bound them up in bales. Then I went down to the riverbank, where I found a noble ship and brand-new about to sail equipped with sails of fine cloth and well manned and provided. So I took passage in her, with a number of other merchants and after embarking our goods, we weighed anchor the same day.

Right fair was our voyage and we sailed from place to place and from isle to isle and whenever we anchored we met a crowd of merchants and notables and customers and we took to buying and selling and bartering. At last destiny brought us to an island, fair and verdant, in trees abundant, with yellow-ripe fruits luxuriant and flowers fragrant and birds warbling soft descant and streams crystalline and radiant. But no sign of man showed to the descrier, not a blower of the fire. The captain made fast with us to this island and the merchants and sailors landed and walked about, enjoying the shade of the trees and the song of the birds, which chanted the praises of the One, the Victorious and marvelling at the works of the Omnipotent King. I landed with the rest and, sitting down by a spring of sweet water that welled up among the trees, took out some vivers I had with me and ate of that which Allah Almighty had allotted unto me. And so sweet was the zephyr and so fragrant were the flowers that presently I waxed drowsy and, lying down in that place, was soon drowned in sleep. When I awoke, I found myself alone, for the ship had sailed and left me behind, nor had one of the merchants or sailors bethought himself of me. I searched the island right and left, but found neither man nor jinn, whereat I was beyond measure troubled and my gall was like to burst for stress of chagrin and anguish and concern, because I was left quite alone, without aught of worldly gear or meat or drink, weary and heartbroken. So I gave myself up for lost and said, "Not always doth the crock escape the shock. I was saved the first time by finding one who brought me from the desert island to an inhabited place, but now there is no hope for me." Then I fell to weeping and wailing and gave myself up to an access of rage, blaming myself for having again ventured upon the perils and hardships of voyage, whenas I was at my ease in mine own house in mine own land, taking my pleasure with good meat and good drink and good clothes and lacking nothing, neither money nor goods. And I repented me of having left Baghdad and this the more after all the travails and dangers I had undergone in my first voyage, wherein I had so narrowly escaped destruction and exclaimed, "Verily we are Allah's and unto Him we are returning!"

I was indeed even as one mad and jinn-struck and presently I rose and walked about the island, right and left and every whither, unable for trouble to sit or tarry in any one place. Then I climbed a tall tree and looked in all directions, but saw nothing save sky and sea and trees and birds and isles and sands. However, after a while my eager glances fell upon some great white thing, afar off in the interior of the island. So I came down from the tree and made for that which I had seen and behold, it was a huge white dome rising high in the air and of vast compass. I walked all around it, but found no door thereto, nor could I muster strength or nimbleness by reason of its exceeding smoothness and slipperiness. So I marked the spot where I stood and went round about the dome to measure its circumference, which I found fifty good paces. And as I stood casting about how to gain an entrance, the day being near its fall and the sun being near the horizon, behold, the sun was suddenly hidden from me and the air became dull and dark. I thought a cloud had come over the sun, but it was the season of summer, so I marvelled at this and, lifting my head, looked steadfastly at the sky, when I saw that the cloud was none other than an enormous bird of gigantic girth and inordinately wide of wing, which as it flew through the air veiled the sun and hid it from the island. At this sight my wonder redoubled and I remembered a story I had heard aforetime of pilgrims and travellers, how in a certain island dwelleth a huge bird, called the "roc", which feedeth its young on elephants and I was certified that the dome which caught my sight was none other than a roc's egg.

As I looked and wondered at the marvellous works of the Almighty, the bird alighted on the dome and brooded over it with its wings covering it and its legs stretched out behind it on the ground and in this posture it fell asleep, glory be to Him who sleepeth not! When I saw this, I arose and, unwinding my turban from my head, doubled it and twisted it into a rope, with which I girt my middle and bound my waist fast to the legs of the roc, saying in myself, "Peradventure this bird may carry me to a land of cities and inhabitants and that will be better than abiding in this desert island." I passed the night watching and fearing to sleep, lest the bird should fly away with me unawares and as soon as the dawn broke and morn shone, the roc rose off its egg and spreading its wings with a great cry, flew up into the air dragging me with it, nor ceased it to soar and to tower until I thought it had reached the limit of the firmament. After which it descended earthward, little by little, until it lighted on the top of a high hill. As soon as I found myself on the hard ground, I made haste to unbind myself, quaking for fear of the bird, though it took no heed of me nor even felt me and loosing my turban from its feet, I made off with my best speed. Presently I saw it catch up in its huge claws something from the earth and rise with it high in air and observing it narrowly, I saw it to be a serpent big of bulk and gigantic of girth, wherewith it flew away clean out of sight. I marvelled at this and faring forward, found myself on a peak overlooking a valley, exceeding great and wide and deep and bounded by vast mountains that spired high in air. None could descry their summits for the excess of their height, nor was any able to climb up thereto. When I saw this, I blamed myself for that which I had done and said, "Would Heaven I had tarried in the island! It was better than this wild desert, for there I had at least fruits to eat and water to drink and here are neither trees nor fruits nor streams. But there is no Majesty and there is no might save in Allah, the Glorious, the Great! Verily, as often as I am quit of one peril I fall into a worse danger and a more grievous." However, I took courage and walking along the wady, found that its soil was of diamond, the stone wherewith they pierce minerals and precious stones and porcelain and onyx, for that it is a dense stone and a dure, whereon neither iron nor hardhed hath effect, neither can we cut off aught there from nor break it, save by means of loadstone. Moreover, the valley swarmed with snakes and vipers, each big as a palm tree, that would have made but one gulp of an elephant. And they came out by night, hiding during the day lest the rocs and eagles pounce on them and tear them to pieces, as was their wont.

And I repented of what I had done, "Allah, I have made haste to bring destruction upon myself!" The day began to wane as I went along and I looked about for a place where I might pass the night, being in fear of the serpents I took no thought of meat and drink in my concern for my life. Presently, I caught sight of a cave near-hand, with a narrow doorway, so I entered and seeing a great stone close to the mouth, I rolled it up and stopped the entrance, saying to myself, "I am safe here for the night and as soon as it is day, I will go forth and see what destiny will do." Then I looked within the cave and saw at the upper end a great serpent brooding on its eggs, at which my flesh quaked and my hair stood on end, but I raised my eyes to Heaven and, committing my case to fate and lot, abode all that night without sleep until daybreak, when I rolled back the stone from the mouth of the cave and went forth, staggering like a drunken man and giddy with watching and fear and hunger. As in this sore case I walked along the valley, behold, there fell down before me a slaughtered beast. But I saw no one, whereat I marvelled with great marvel and presently remembered a story I had heard aforetime from traders and pilgrims and travellers about diamond mountains which are full of perils and terrors, nor can any fare through them, but the merchants who traffic in diamonds have a

device by which they obtain them, that is to say, they take a sheep and slaughter and skin it and cut it in pieces and cast them down from the mountaintops into the valley sole, where, the meat being fresh and sticky with blood, some of the gems cleave to it. Then they leave it until midday, when the eagles and vultures swoop down upon it and carry it in their claws to the mountain summits, whereupon the merchants come and shout at them and scare them away from the meat. Then they come and taking the diamonds which they find sticking to it, go their ways with them and leave the meat to the birds and beasts, nor can any come at the diamonds but by this device.

So when I saw the slaughtered beast fall bethought me of the story, I went up to it and filled my pockets and shawl girdle and turban and the folds of my clothes with the choicest diamonds and as I was thus engaged, down fell before me another great piece of meat. Then with my unrolled turban and lying on my back, I set the bit on my breast so that I was hidden by the meat, which was thus raised above the ground. Hardly had I gripped it when an eagle swooped down upon the flesh and, seizing it with its talons, flew up with it high in air and me clinging thereto and ceased not its flight until it alighted on the head of one of the mountains, where, dropping the carcass it fell to rending it. But, behold, there arose behind it a great noise of shouting and clattering of wood, whereat the bird took fright and flew away. Then I loosed off myself the meat, with clothes daubed with blood there from and stood up by its side. Whereupon up came the merchant who had cried out at the eagle and seeing me standing there, bespoke me not, but was affrighted at me and shook with fear. However, he went up to the carcass and, turning it over, found no diamonds sticking to it, whereat he gave a great cry and exclaimed, "Harrow, my disappointment! There is no Majesty and there is no might save in Allah with whom we seek refuge from Satan the stoned!" And he bemoaned himself and beat hand upon hand, saying, "Alas, the pity of it! How cometh this?"

Then I went up to him and he said to me, "Who art thou and what causeth thee to come hither?"

And I, "Fear not, I am a man and a good man and a merchant. My story is a wondrous and my adventures marvellous and the manner of my coming hither is prodigious. So be of good cheer. Thou shalt receive of me what shall rejoice thee, for I have with me great plenty of diamonds and I will give thee thereof what shall suffice thee, for each is better than aught thou couldst get otherwise. So fear nothing."

The man rejoiced thereat and thanked and blessed me. Then we talked together until the other merchants, hearing me in discourse with their fellow, came up and saluted me, for each of them had thrown down his piece of meat. And as I went off with them and told them my whole story, how I had suffered hardships at sea and the fashion of my reaching the valley. But I gave the owner of the meat a number of the stones I had by me, so they all wished me joy of my escape, saying, "By Allah, a new life hath been decreed to thee, for none ever reached yonder valley and came off thence alive before thee, but praised be Allah for thy safety!" We passed the night together in a safe and pleasant place, beyond measure rejoiced at my deliverance from the valley of serpents and my arrival in an inhabited land.

And on the morrow we set out and journeyed over the mighty range of mountains, seeing many serpents in the valley, until we came to a fair great island wherein was a garden of huge champhor trees under each of which a hundred men might take shelter. Moreover, there is in this island a kind of wild beast, called a rhinoceros, which pastureth as do steers and buffaloes with us, but it is a huge brute, bigger of body than the camel and like it feedeth upon the leaves and twigs of trees. Voyagers and pilgrims and travellers declare that this beast called karkadan will carry off a great elephant on

its horn and graze about the island and the seacoast therewith and take no heed of it until the elephant dieth and its fat, melting in the sun, runneth down into the rhinoceros' eyes and blindeth him, so that he lieth down on the shore. Then comes the bird roc and carrieth off both the rhinoceros and that which is on its horn, to feed its young withal. Moreover, I saw in this island many kinds of oxen and buffaloes whose like are not found in our country. Here I sold some of the diamonds which I had by me for gold dinars and silver dirhams and bartered others for the produce of the country and loading them upon beasts of burden, fared on with the merchants from valley to valley and town to town, buying and selling and viewing foreign countries and the works and creatures of Allah until we came to Bassorah city, where we abode a few days, after which I continued my journey to Baghdad.

I arrived at home with great store of diamonds and money and goods and forgathered with my friends and relations and gave alms and largess and bestowed curious gifts and made presents to all my friends and companions. Then I betook myself to eating well and drinking well and wearing fine clothes and making merry with my fellows and forgot all my sufferings in the pleasures of return to the solace and delight of life, with light heart and broadened breast. And everyone who heard of my return came and questioned me of my adventures and of foreign countries and I related to them all that had befallen me and the much I had suffered, whereat they wondered and gave me joy of my safe return. This, then, is the end of the story of my second voyage and tomorrow, Inshallah! I will tell you what befell me in my third voyage. The company marvelled at his story and supped with him, after which he ordered a hundred dinars of gold to be given to the porter, who took the sum with many thanks and blessings and went his way, wondering at what he had heard. Next morning as soon as day came in its sheen and shone, he rose and, praying the dawn prayer, repaired to the house of Sindbad the Seaman and went in and gave him good morrow. The merchant welcomed him and made him sit with him until the rest of the company arrived and when they had well eaten and drunken and were merry with joy and jollity, their host began by saying, "Hearken, O my brothers, to what I am about to tell you, for it is even more wondrous than what you have already heard. Listen to the Third Voyage of Sindbad the Seaman."

84

The Third Voyage of Sindbad the Seaman

Illustrated by Dr. Alderete & El Valiente

As I told you yesterday, I returned from my second voyage overjoyed at my safety and with great increase of wealth, Allah having requited me all that I had wasted and lost, and I abode awhile in Baghdad city savouring the utmost ease and prosperity and comfort and happiness, until the carnal man was once more seized with longing for travel and diversion and adventure and yearned after traffic and lucre and emolument, for the human heart is naturally prone to evil. So, making up my mind, I laid in great plenty of goods suitable for a sea voyage and repairing to Bassorah, went down to the shore and found there a fine ship ready to sail with a full crew and a numerous company of merchants, men of worth and substance, faith, piety and consideration. I embarked with them and we set sail on the blessing of Allah Almighty and on His aidance and His favour to bring our voyage to a safe and prosperous issue and already we congratulated one another on our good fortune and boon voyage. We fared on from sea to sea and from island to island and city to city, in all delight and contentment, buying and selling wherever we touched and taking our solace and our pleasure, until one day when as we sailed athwart the dashing sea swollen with clashing billows, behold, the master, who stood on the gunwale examining the ocean in all directions, cried out with a great cry and buffeted his face and pluckt out his beard and rent his raiment and bade furl the sail and cast the anchors. So we said to him, "O Rais, what is the matter?"

"Know, O my brethren that the wind hath gotten the better of us and hath driven us out of our course into mid-ocean and destiny, for our ill luck, hath brought us to the Mountain of the Zughb, a hairy people like apes, among whom no man ever fell and came forth alive. And my heart presageth that we all be dead men."

Hardly had the master made an end of his speech when the apes were upon us. They surrounded the ship on all sides, swarming like locusts and crowding the shore. They were the most frightful of wild creatures, covered with black hair like felt, foul of favour and small of stature, being but four spans high, yellow-eyed and black-faced. None knoweth their language nor what they are and they shun the company of men. We feared to slay them or strike them or drive them away, because of their inconceivable multitude, lest if we hurt one, the rest fall on us and slay us, for numbers prevail over courage. So we let them do their will, albeit we feared they would plunder our goods and gear. They swarmed up the cables and gnawed them asunder and on likewise they did with all the ropes of the ship, so that it fell off from the wind and stranded upon their mountainous coast. Then they laid hands on all the merchants and crew and landing us on the island, made off with the ship and its cargo and went their ways.

We were thus left on the island, eating of its fruits and potherbs and drinking of its streams until one day we espied in its midst what seemed an inhabited house. So we made for it as fast as our feet could carry us and, behold, it was a castle strong and tall, compassed about with a lofty wall and having a two-leaved gate of ebony wood, both of which open stood. We entered and found within a space wide and bare like a great square, around which stood many high doors open thrown and at the further end a long bench of stone and brazier with cooking gear hanging thereon and about it great plenty of bones. But we saw no one and marvelled thereat with exceeding wonder.

Then we sat down in the courtyard a little while and presently falling asleep, slept from the forenoon until sundown, when suddenly the earth trembled under our feet and the air rumbled with a terrible tone. Then there came down upon us, from the top of the castle, a huge creature in the likeness of a man, black of colour, tall and big of bulk, as if he were a great date tree, with eyes like coals of fire and eyeteeth like a boar's tusks and a vast big gape like the mouth of a well. Moreover, he had long loose lips like a camel's hanging down upon his breast and ears like two jarms falling over his shoulder blades and the nails of his hands were like the claws of a lion. When we saw this frightful giant, we were like to faint and every moment increased our fear and terror and we became as dead men for excess of horror and affright. And after trampling upon the earth, he sat awhile on the bench. Then he arose and coming to us, seized me by the arm, choosing me from among my comrades the merchants. He took me up in his hand and turning me over, felt me as a butcher feeleth a sheep he is about to slaughter and I but a little mouthful in his hands. But finding me lean and fleshless for stress of toil and trouble and weariness, let me go and took up another, whom in like manner he turned over and

felt and let go. Nor did he cease to feel and turn over the rest of us, one after another, until he came to the master of the ship. Now he was a sturdy, stout, broad-shouldered wight, fat and in full vigour, so he pleased the giant, who seized him as a butcher seizeth a beast and throwing him down, set his foot on his neck and broke it. Then, lighting a fierce fire, he set over it a spit with the Rais thereon and turned it over the coals until the flesh was roasted. Then he tore the body, limb from limb, as one jointeth a chicken and, rending the flesh with his nails, fell to eating of it and gnawing the bones, until there was nothing left but some of these, which he threw on one side of the wall. This done, he sat for a while, then he lay down on the stone bench and fell asleep, snoring like the gurgling of a lamb or a cow with its throat cut, nor did he awake until morning, when he rose and fared forth and went his ways.

As soon as we were certified that he was gone, we began to talk with one another, weeping and bemoaning ourselves for the risk we ran and saying, "Would Heaven we had been drowned in the sea or that the apes had eaten us! That were better than to be roasted over the coals. By Allah, this is a vile, foul death! But whatso the Lord willeth must come-to pass and there is no Majesty and there is no might save in Him, the

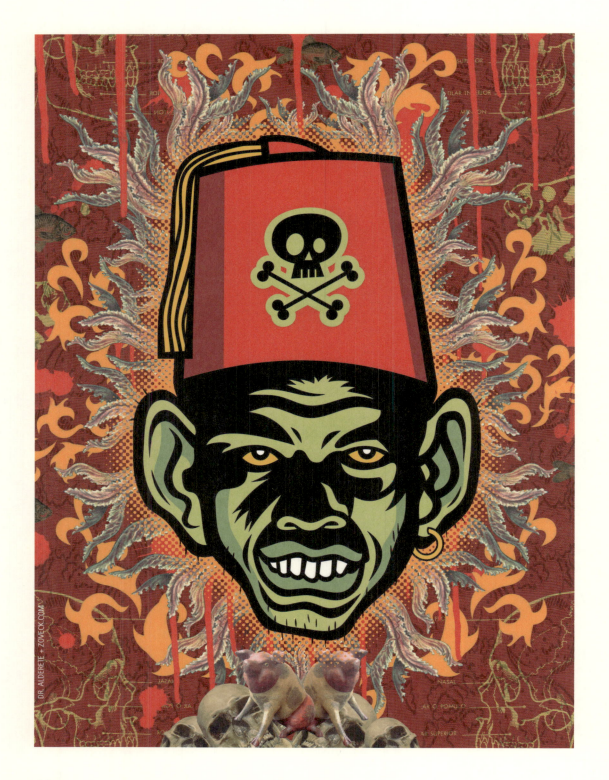

Glorious, the Great! We shall assuredly perish miserably and none will know of us, as there is no escape for us from this place."

Then we arose and roamed about the island, hoping that haply we might find a place to hide or a means of flight, for indeed death was a light matter to us, provided we were not roasted over the fire and eaten. However, we could find no hiding place and the evening overtook us, so, of the excess of our terror, we returned to the castle and sat down awhile. Presently, the earth trembled under our feet and the ogre came up to us and turning us over, felt one after other until he found a man to his liking, whom he took and served as he had done the captain, killing and roasting and eating him. After which he lay down on the bench and slept snoring like a beast with its throat cut, until daybreak, when he arose and went out as before. Then we drew together and conversed and added one to the other, "By Allah, we had better throw ourselves into the sea and be drowned than die roasted for this is an abominable death!" Quoth one of us, "Hear ye my words! Let us cast about to kill him and be at peace from the grief of him and rid the Moslems of his barbarity and tyranny."

Then said I, "Hear me, O my brothers. If there is nothing for it but to slay him, let us carry some of this firewood and planks down to the seashore and make us a boat wherein, if we succeed in slaughtering him, we may either embark and let the waters carry us whither Allah willeth, or else abide here until some ship passes, when we will take passage in it. If we fail to kill him, we will embark in the boat and put out to sea. And if we be drowned, we shall at least escape being roasted over a kitchen fire, whilst if we escape, we escape and if we be drowned, we die martyrs."

"By Allah," said they all, "this rede is a right," and we agreed upon this and set about carrying it out. So we haled down to the beach the pieces of wood which lay about the bench and making a boat, moored it to the strand, after which we stowed therein somewhat of victual and returned to the castle.

As soon as evening fell the earth trembled under our feet and in came the beast upon us, snarling like a dog about to bite. He came up to us and feeling us and turning us over one by one, took one of us and did with him as he had done before and ate him, after which he lay down on the bench and snored and snorted like thunder. As soon as we were assured that he slept, we arose and taking two iron spits of those standing there, heated them in the fiercest of the fire until they were red-hot, like burning coals, when we gripped fast hold of them and going up to the giant as he lay snoring on the bench, thrust them into his eyes and pressed upon them, all of us, with our united might, so that his eyeballs burst and he became stone-blind. Thereupon he cried with a great cry, whereat our hearts trembled and springing up from the bench, he fell a-groping after us, blindfolded. We fled from him right and left and he saw us not, for his sight was altogether gone, but we were in terrible fear of him and made sure we were dead men despairing of escape.

Then he found the door, feeling for it with his hands and went out roaring aloud and behold, the earth shook under us for the noise of his roaring and we quaked for fear. As he quitted the castle we followed him and betook ourselves to the place where we had moored our boat, saying to one another, "If this accursed abide is absent until the going down of the sun and comes not to the castle, we shall know that he is dead, and if he come back, we will embark in the boat and paddle until we escape, committing our affair to Allah." But as we spoke, behold, up came the beast with other two as they were Ghuls, fouler and more frightful than he, with eyes like red-hot coals, which when we saw, we hurried into the boat and casting off the moorings, paddled away and pushed out to sea. As soon as the ogres caught sight of us, they cried out at us and running down to the sea-shore, fell a-pelting us with rocks, whereof some fell amongst us and others fell into the sea. We paddled with all our might until we were beyond their reach, but the most part of us were slain by the rock-throwing and the winds and waves sported with us and carried us into the midst of the dashing sea, swollen with billows clashing. We knew not whither we went and my fellows died one after another until there remained but three, myself and two others, for as often as one died, we threw him into the sea. We were sore exhausted for stress of hunger, but we took courage and heartened one another and worked for dear life and paddled with might until the winds cast us upon an island, as we were dead men for fatigue and fear and famine. We landed on the island and walked about it for a while, finding that it abounded in trees and streams and birds and we ate of the fruits and rejoiced in our escape from the giant and our deliverance from the perils of the sea. And thus we did until nightfall, when we lay down and fell asleep for excess of fatigue. But we had hardly closed our eyes before we were aroused by a hissing sound, like the sough of wind and awakening, we saw a serpent like a dragon, a seldseen sight, of monstrous make and belly of enormous bulk, which lay in a circle around us. Presently it reared its head and seizing one of my companions, swallowed him up to his shoulders. Then it gulped down the rest of him and we heard his ribs crack in its belly. Presently it went its way and we

abode in sore amazement and grief for our comrade and mortal fear for ourselves, saying, "By Allah, this is a marvellous thing! Each kind of death that threateneth us is more terrible than the last. We were rejoicing in our escape from the ogre and our deliverance from the perils of the sea, but now we have fallen into that which is worse. There is no Majesty and there is no Might save in Allah! By the Almighty, we have escaped from the giant and from drowning, but how shall we escape from this abominable and viperish monster?"

Then we walked about the island, eating of its fruits and drinking of its streams until dusk, when we climbed up into a high tree and went to sleep there, I being on the top-most bough. As soon as it was dark night, up came the serpent, looking right and left and making for the tree whereon we were, climbed up to my comrade and swallowed him down to his shoulders. Then it coiled about the bole with him, whilst I, who could not take my eyes off the sight, heard his bones crack in its belly and it swallowed him whole, after which it slid down from the tree. When the day broke and the light showed me that the serpent was gone, I came down, as I were a dead man for stress of fear and anguish and thought to cast myself into the sea and be at rest from the woes of the world, but could not bring myself to this, for verily life is dear.

So I took five pieces of wood, broad and long and bound one crosswise to the soles of my feet and others in like fashion on my right and left sides and over my breast and the broadest and largest I bound across my head and made them fast with ropes. Then I lay down on the ground on my back, so that I was completely fenced in by the pieces of wood, which enclosed me. So as soon as it was dark, up came the serpent as usual and made toward me, but could not get at me to swallow me for the wood that fenced me in. So it wriggled round me on every side whilst I looked on like one dead by reason of my terror and every now and then it would glide away and then come back. But as often as it tried to come at me, it was hindered by the pieces of wood wherewith I had bound myself on every side. It ceased not to beset me thus from sundown until dawn, but when the light of day shone upon the beast it made off, in the utmost fury and extreme disappointment. Then I put out my hand and unbound myself, well-nigh down among the dead men for fear and suffering and went down to the island shore, whence a ship afar off in the midst of the waves suddenly struck my sight. So I tore off a great branch of a tree and made signs with it to the crew, shouting out the while, which when the ship's company saw they said to one another, "We must stand in and see what this is. Peradventure 'tis a man."

So they made for the island and presently heard my cries, whereupon they took me on board and questioned me of my case. I told them all my adventures from first to last, whereat they marvelled mightily and covered my shame with some of their clothes. Moreover, they set before me somewhat of food and I ate my fill and I drank cold sweet water and was mightily refreshed and Allah Almighty quickened me after I was virtually dead. So I praised the Most Highest and thanked Him for His favours and exceeding mercies and my heart revived in me after utter despair, until it seemed as if all I had suffered were but a dream I had dreamed.

We sailed on with a fair wind the Almighty sent us until we came to an island called Al-Salahitah, which aboundeth in sandalwood, when the captain cast anchor. And when we had cast anchor, the merchants and the sailors landed with their goods to sell and to buy. Then the captain turned to me and said, "Hark'ee, thou art a stranger and a pauper and tellest us that thou hast undergone frightful hardships, wherefore I have a mind to benefit thee with somewhat that may further thee to thy native land, so thou wilt ever bless me and pray for me."

"So be it," answered I. "Thou shalt have my prayers."

Quoth he, "Know then that there was with us a man, a traveller, whom we lost and we

DR. ALDERETE + ZOVECK.COM

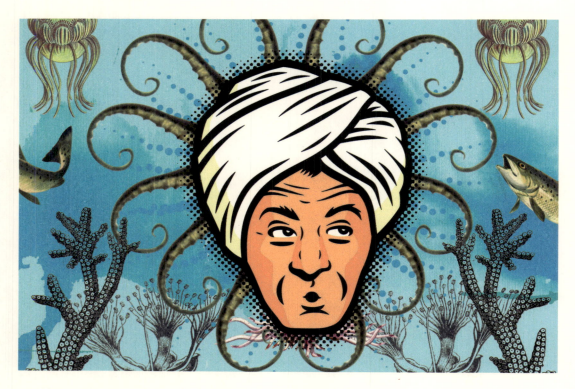

know not if he be alive or dead, for we had no news of him. So I purpose to commit his bales of goods to thy charge, so that thou mayst sell them in this island. A part of the proceeds we will give thee as an equivalent for thy pains and service and the rest we will keep until we return to Baghdad, where we will inquire for his family and deliver it to them, together with the unsold goods. Say me then, wilt thou undertake the charge and land and sell them as other merchants do?"

I replied, "Hearkening and obedience to thee, O my lord and great is thy kindness to me," and thanked him. Whereupon he bade the sailors and porters to bear the bales in question ashore and commit them to my charge.

The ship's scribe asked him, "O master, what bales are these and what merchant's name shall I write upon them?" and he answered, "Write on them the name of Sindbad the Seaman, him who was with us in the ship and whom we lost at the roc's island and of whom we have no tidings. For we mean this stranger to sell them and we will give him a part of the price for his pains and keep the rest until we return to Baghdad, where if we find the owner we will make it over to him and if not, to his family." And the clerk said, "Thy words are apposite and thy rede is right."

Now when I heard the captain give orders for the bales to be inscribed with my name, I said to myself, "By Allah, I am Sindbad the Seaman!" So I armed myself with courage and patience and waited until all the merchants had landed and were gathered together, talking and chattering about buying and selling. Then I went up to the captain and asked him, "O my lord, knowest thou what manner of man was this Sindbad whose goods thou hast committed to me for sale?" and he answered, "I know of him naught save that he was a man from Baghdad city, Sindbad hight the Seaman, who was drowned with many others when we lay anchored at such an island and I have heard nothing of him since then."

At this I cried out with a great cry and said, "O Captain, whom Allah keep! Know that I am that Sindbad the Seaman and that I was not drowned, but when thou castest anchor at the island, I landed with the rest of the merchants and crew. And I sat down in a pleasant place by myself and ate somewhat of food I had with me and enjoyed myself until I became drowsy and was drowned in sleep. And when I awoke, I found no ship and none near me. These goods are my goods and these bales are my bales and all the merchants who fetch jewels from the Valley of Diamonds saw me there and will bear me witness that I am the very Sindbad the Seaman, for I related to them everything that had befallen me and told them how you forgot me and left me sleeping on the island." When the passengers and crew heard my words, they gathered about me and some of them believed me and others disbelieved, but presently, behold, one of the merchants, hearing me mention the Valley of Diamonds, came up to me and said to them, "Hear what I say, good people! When I related to you the most wonderful things in my travels and I told you that at the time we cast down our slaughtered animals into the Valley of Serpents, there came up a man hanging to mine, ye believed me not and live me the lie."

"Yes," quoth they, "thou didst tell us some such tale, but we had no call to credit thee." He resumed, "Now this is the very man, by token that he gave me diamonds of great value and high price whose like are not to be found, requiting me more than would have come up sticking to my quarter of meat. And I companied with him to Bassorah city, where he took leave of us and went on to his native stead whilst we returned to our own land. This is he and he told us his name, Sindbad the Seaman and how the ship left him on the desert island. And know ye that Allah hath sent him hither, so might the truth of my story be made manifest to you. Moreover, these are his goods, for when he first forgathered with us, he told us of them, and the truth of his words is patent."

Hearing the merchant's speech, the captain came up to me and considered me awhile, after which he said, "What was the mark on thy bales?"

"Thus and thus," answered I and reminded him of somewhat that had passed between him and me when I shipped with him from Bassorah.

Thereupon he was convinced that I was indeed Sindbad the Seaman and took me round the neck and gave me joy of my safety, saying, "By Allah, O my lord, thy case is indeed wondrous and thy tale marvellous. But lauded be Allah, who hath brought thee and me together again and who hath restored to thee thy goods and gear!"

Then I disposed of my merchandise to the best of my skill and profited largely on them, whereat I rejoiced with exceeding joy and congratulated myself on my safety and the recovery of my goods.

Then we set sail again with a fair wind and the blessing of Almighty Allah and after a prosperous voyage, arrived safe and sound at Bassorah. Here I abode a few days and presently returned to Baghdad, where I went at once to my quarter and my house and saluted my family and friends. I had gained on this voyage what was beyond count and reckoning, so I gave alms and largess and clad the widow and orphan, by way of thanksgiving for my happy return and fell to feasting and making merry with my companions and intimates and forgot while eating well and drinking well and dressing well everything that had befallen me and all the perils and hardships I had suffered. These, then, are the most admirable things I sighted on my third voyage and tomorrow, be it the will of Allah, you shall come to me and I will relate the adventures of my fourth voyage, which is even more wonderful than those you have already heard. Then Sindbad the Seaman bade to give Sindbad the Landsman a hundred golden dinars as of wont and called for food. So they spread the tables and the company ate the night meal and went their ways, marvelling at the tale they had heard.

The porter after taking his gold passed the night in his own house, also wondering at what his namesake the seaman had told him and as soon as day broke and the morning showed with its sheen and shone, he rose and praying the dawn prayer, betook himself to Sindbad the Seaman, who returned his salute and received him with an open breast and cheerful favour and made him sit with him until the rest of the company arrived, when he caused to set on food and they ate and drank and made merry. Then Sindbad the Seaman bespoke them and related to them the narrative of the Fourth Voyage of Sindbad the Seaman.

98

The Fourth Voyage of Sindbad the Seaman

Illustrated by Jules Langran

Know, O my brethren, that after my return from my third voyage and forgathering with my friends and forgetting all my perils and hardships in the enjoyment of ease and comfort and repose, I was visited one day by a company of merchants who sat down with me and talked of foreign travel and traffic until the old bad man within me yearned to go with them and enjoy the sight of strange countries and I longed for the society of the various races of mankind and for traffic and profit. So I resolved to travel with them and, buying the necessaries for a long voyage and great store of costly goods, more than ever before, transported them from Baghdad to Bassorah, where I took ship with the merchants in question.

We set out, trusting in the blessing of Almighty Allah and with a favouring breeze and the best conditions we sailed from island to island and sea to sea until one day there arose against us a contrary wind and the captain cast out his anchors and brought the ship to a standstill, fearing lest she should founder in mid-ocean. Then we all fell to prayer and humbling ourselves before the Most High, but as we were thus engaged there smote us a furious squall which tore the sails to rags and tatters. The anchor cable parted and, the ship foundering, we were cast into the sea, goods and all. I kept myself afloat by swimming half the day until, when I had given myself up for lost, the Almighty threw in my way one of the planks of the ship, whereon I and some others of the merchants scrambled and, mounting it as we would a horse, paddled with our feet in the sea. We abode thus a day and a night, the wind and waves helping us on and on the second day shortly before midday the breeze freshened and the sea wrought and the rising waves cast us upon an island. We walked about the shore and found abundance of herbs, whereof we ate enough to keep breath in body and to stay our failing spirits, then lay down and slept until morning hard by the sea. And when morning came with its sheen and shone, we arose

and walked about the island to the right and left until we came in sight of an inhabited house afar off. So we made toward it and ceased not walking until we reached the door thereof, when suddenly, a number of naked men issued from it and without saluting us or a word said, laid hold of us masterfully and carried us to their King, who signed us to sit. So we sat down and they set food before us such as we knew not and whose like we had never seen in all our lives. My companions ate of it, for stress of hunger, but my stomach revolted from it and I would not eat and my refraining from it was, by Allah's favour, the cause of my being alive until now. For no sooner had my comrades tasted of it than their reason fled and their condition changed and they began to devour it like madmen possessed of an evil spirit. Then the savages gave them to drink of coconut oil and anointed them therewith and straightway after drinking thereof their eyes turned into their heads and they fell to eating greedily, against their wont.

When I saw this I was extremely confused and concerned for them, nor was I less anxious about myself, for fear of the naked people. So I watched them narrowly and it was not long before I discovered them to be a tribe of Magian cannibals whose King was a Ghul. All who came to their country or whoso they caught in their valleys or on their roads they brought to this King and fed them upon that food and anointed them with that oil, whereupon their stomachs dilated that they might eat largely. Then they stuffed them with coconut oil and the aforesaid food until they became fat and gross, when they slaughtered them by cutting their throats and roasted them for the King's eating, but as for the savages themselves, they ate human flesh raw. When I saw this, I was sore dismayed for myself and my comrades, who were now so stupefied that they knew not what was done with them. And the naked people committed them to one who used every day to lead them out and pasture them on the island like cattle. And they wandered amongst the trees and rested at will, thus waxing very fat.

As for me, I wasted away and became sickly for fear and hunger and my flesh shrivelled on my bones, which when the savages saw, they left me alone and took no thought of me and so far forgot me that one day I gave them the slip and walking out of their place, made for the beach, which was distant and there espied a very old man seated on a high place girt by the waters. I looked at him and knew him for the herdsman who had charge of pasturing my fellows and with him were many others in like case. As soon as he saw me, he knew me to be in possession of my reason and not afflicted like the rest whom he was pasturing, so signed to me from afar, as who should say, "Turn back and take the right-hand road, for that will lead thee into the King's highway." So I turned back, as he bade me and followed the right-hand road, now running for fear and then walking leisurely to rest me, until I was out of the old man's sight. By this time the sun had gone down and the darkness set in, so I sat down to rest and would have slept, but sleep came not to me that night for stress of fear and famine and fatigue. When the night was half spent, I rose and walked on until the day broke in all its beauty and the sun rose over the heads of the lofty hills and athwart the low gravely plains.

I did not I cease walking for seven days and their nights, until the morn of the eighth day, when I caught sight of a faint object in the distance. So I made toward it, though my heart quaked for all I had suffered first and last and, behold, it was a company of men gathering pepper grains. As soon as they saw me, they hastened up to me and surrounding me on all sides, said to me, "Who art thou and whence come?"

I replied, "Know, O people, that I am a poor stranger," and acquainted them with my case and all the hardships and perils I had suffered, whereat they marvelled and gave me joy of my safety.

And after I had told them the fate of my companions, they made me sit by them until they got quit of their work and fetched me somewhat of good food, which I ate, for I was hungry and rested awhile. After which they took ship with me and carrying me to their island home, brought me before their King, who returned my salute and received me honourably and questioned me of my case. I told him all that had befallen me from the day of my leaving Baghdad city, whereupon he wondered with great wonder at my adventures and bade me to sit by him. Then he called for food and I ate with him what sufficed me and washed my hands and returned thanks to Almighty Allah for all His favours, praising Him and glorifying Him. Then I left the King and walked for solace about the city, which I found wealthy and populous. So I rejoiced at having reached so pleasant a place and took my ease there, nor was it long before I became more in honour and favour with the people and their King.

Now I saw that all the citizens, great and small, rode fine horses, high-priced and thoroughbred, without saddles or housings, whereat I wondered and said to the King, "Wherefore, O my lord, dost thou not ride with a saddle? Therein is ease for the rider and increase of power."

"What is a saddle?" asked he, "I have never seen nor used such a thing in all my life." And I answered, "With thy permission I will make thee a saddle, that thou mayst ride on it and see the comfort thereof."

And quoth he, "Do so."

So quoth I to him, "Furnish me with some woods." which being brought, I sought me a clever carpenter and sitting by him, showed him how to make the saddletree. Then I took wool and teased it and made felt of it and, covering the saddletree with leather, stuffed it, polished it and attached the girth and stirrup leathers. After which I fetched a blacksmith and described to him the fashion of the stirrups and bridle bit. So he forged a fine pair of stirrups and a bit and filed them smooth and tinned them. Moreover, I made fast to them fringes of silk and fitted bridle leathers to the bit. Then I fetched one of the best of the royal horses and saddling and bridling it, hung the stirrups to the saddle and led him to the King.

The thing took his fancy and he thanked me, then he mounted and rejoiced greatly in the saddle and rewarded me handsomely for my work. When the King's Vizir saw the saddle, he asked of me one like it and I made it for him. Furthermore, all the grandees and officers came for saddles to me, so I fell to making saddles and selling them to all who sought one.

103

I abode thus until one day, as I was sitting with the King in all respect and contentment, he said to me, "Know thou art become one of us, dear as a brother and we hold thee in such regard and affection that we cannot part with thee nor suffer thee to leave our city. Wherefore I desire of thee obedience in a certain matter and I will not have thee gainsay me."

Answered I, "O King, what is it thou desirest of me? Far be it from me to gainsay thee in aught, for I am indebted to thee for many favours and bounties and much kindness and I have become one of thy servants."

Quoth he, "I have a mind to marry thee to a fair, clever and agreeable wife who is as wealthy as she is beautiful, so thou mayest be naturalised and domiciled with us."

So he summoned the kazi and the witnesses and married me straightway to a lady of a noble tree and high pedigree, wealthy in moneys and means.

Now after the King my master had married me to this choice wife, he also gave me a great and goodly house standing alone, together with slaves and officers and assigned me pay and allowances. So I became in all ease and contentment and delight and forgot everything which had befallen me of weariness and trouble and hardship. I loved my wife with fondest love and she loved me no less and we were as one and abode in the utmost comfort of life. And I said in myself, "When I return to my native land, I will carry her with me."

We lived thus a great while, until Almighty Allah bereft one of my neighbours of his wife. Now he was a gossip of mine, so hearing the cry of the keeners, I went in to condole with him on his loss and found him in very ill plight, full of trouble and weary of soul and mind. I condoled with him and comforted him, saying, "Mourn not for thy wife, who hath now found the mercy of Allah."

But he wept bitter tears and replied, "O my friend, how shall Allah replace her to me with a better than she, when I have but one day left to live?"

"O my brother," said I, "return to thy senses and announce not glad tidings of thine own death, for thou art well, sound and in good case."

"By thy life, O my friend," rejoined he, "tomorrow thou wilt lose me and wilt never see me again until the Day of Resurrection."

I asked, "How so?" and he answered, "This very day they bury my wife and they bury me with her in one tomb. For it is the custom with us, if the wife dies first, to bury the husband alive with her and in like manner the wife if the husband dies first, so that neither may enjoy life after losing his or her mate."

"By Allah," cried I, "this is a most vile, lewd custom and not to be endured of any!" Meanwhile, behold, the most part of the townsfolk came in and laid the dead woman out, as was their wont and setting her on a bier, carried her and her husband until they came to a place in the side of a mountain at the end of the island by the sea. And here they raised a great rock and discovered the mouth of a pit, leading down into a vast underground cavern that ran beneath the mountain. Into this pit they threw the corpse, then, tying a rope of palm fibres under the husband's armpits, they let him down into the cavern and with him a great pitcher of fresh water and seven scones. When he came to the bottom, he loosed himself from the rope and they drew it up and stopping the mouth of the pit with the great stone, they returned to the city, leaving my friend in the cavern with his dead wife. When I saw this, I said to myself, "By Allah, this fashion of death is more grievous than the first!" And I went to the King and said to him, "O my lord, why do ye bury the living with the dead?"

Quoth he, "It hath been the custom, thou must know, of our ancestors, if the husband dies first, to bury his wife with him and the like with the wife, so we may not sever them, alive or dead."

I asked, "O King of the Age, if the wife of a foreigner like myself dies, deal ye with him as with yonder man?" and he answered, "Assuredly we do with him even as thou hast seen."

When I heard this, my gall bladder was like to burst for the violence of my dismay and concern for myself. I felt as if in a vile dungeon and hated their society, for I went about in fear lest my wife should die before me and they bury me alive with her. However, after a while I comforted myself, saying, "Haply I shall predecease her or shall have returned to my own land before she dies, for none knoweth which shall go first and which shall go last." Then I applied myself to diverting my mind from this thought with various occupations, but it was not long before my wife sickened and complained and took to her bed, and fared after a few days to the mercy of Allah. And the King and the rest of the people came, as was their wont, to condole with me and her family and to console us for her loss and not less to condole with me for myself.

Then the women washed her and arraying her in her richest raiment and golden ornaments, necklaces and jewellery, laid her on the bier and bore her to the mountain aforesaid, where they lifted the cover of the pit and cast her in. After which all my intimates and acquaintances and my wife's kith and kin came round me, to farewell me in my lifetime and console me for my own death, whilst I cried out among them, saying, "Almighty Allah never made it lawful to bury the living with the dead!" They heard me not and paid no heed to my words, but laying hold of me, bound me by force and let me down into the cavern with a large pitcher of sweet water and seven cakes of bread, according to their custom. When I came to the bottom, they called out to me to cast myself loose from the cords, but I refused to do so, so they threw them down on me and, closing the mouth of the pit with the stones aforesaid, went their ways. I looked about me and found myself in a vast cave full of dead bodies that exhaled a fulsome and loathsome smell and the air was heavy with the groans of the dying. Thereupon I fell to blaming myself for what I had done, saying, "By Allah, I deserve all that hath befallen me and all that shall befall me!" Then I threw myself down on the bones of the dead and lay there, imploring Allah's help and in the violence of my despair invoking death, which came not to me. After this, the worst night I ever knew, I arose and exploring the cavern, found that it extended a long way with hollows in its sides and that its floor was strewn with dead bodies and rotten bones. So I made myself a place in a cavity of the cavern, afar from the corpses lately thrown down and slept there. I abode thus a long

while, until my provision was like to give out and yet I ate not save once every day or second day, nor did I drink more than an occasional draught, for fear my victual should fail me before my death. And I said to myself, "Eat little and drink little!"

One day as I sat thus, pondering my case and bethinking me how I should do when my bread and water should be exhausted, behold, the stone that covered the opening was suddenly rolled away and the light streamed down upon me. Quoth I, "I wonder what is the matter. Haply they have brought another corpse." Then I espied people standing about the mouth of the pit, who presently let down a dead man and a live woman, weeping and bemoaning herself and with her an ampler supply of bread and water than usual. I saw her, but she saw me not. And they closed up the opening and went away. Then I took the leg bone of a dead man and, going up to the woman, smote her on the crown of the head and she cried one cry and fell down dead. When I laid hands on her bread and water and found on her great plenty of ornaments and rich apparel, necklaces, jewels and gold trinkets, for it was their custom to bury women in all their finery. I carried the vivers to my sleeping place in the cavern side and ate and drank of them sparingly.

I abode thus a great while, killing all the live people they let down into the cavern and taking their provisions of meat and drink, until one day, as I slept, I was awakened by something scratching and burrowing among the bodies in a corner of the cave and said, "What can this be?" fearing wolves or hyenas. So I sprang up and seizing the leg bone aforesaid, made for the noise. As soon as the thing was ware of me, it fled from me into the inward of the cavern. However, I followed it to the further end, until I saw afar off a point of light not bigger than a star, now appearing and then disappearing. So I made for it and as I drew near, it grew larger and brighter, until I was certified that it was a crevice in the rock, leading to the open country and I said to myself, "There must be some reason for this opening. Either it is the mouth of a second pit such as that by which they let me down or else it is a natural fissure in the stone." So I bethought me awhile and nearing the light, found that it came from a breach at the rear of the mountain, which the wild beasts had enlarged by burrowing, so that they might enter and devour the dead and freely go to and from. When I saw this, my spirits revived and hope came back to me and I made sure of life, after having died a death. So I went on and found myself on the slope of a high mountain overlooking the salt sea and cutting off all access thereto from the island, so that none could come at that part of the beach from the city.

Then I returned through the crack to the cavern and brought out all the food and water I had saved up and donned some of the dead people's clothes over my own. After which I gathered together all the collars and necklaces of pearls and jewels and trinkets of gold and silver set with precious stones and other ornaments and valuables I could find upon the corpses and making them into bundles with the clothes and raiment of the dead, carried them out to the back of the mountain facing the seashore, where I established myself, purposing to wait there until it should please Almighty Allah to send me relief by means of some passing ship. I visited the cavern daily and as often as I found people buried alive there, I killed them all indifferently, men and women and took their victual and valuables and transported them to my seat on the seashore.

Thus I abode a long while until one day I caught sight of a ship passing in the midst of the clashing sea swollen with dashing billows. So I took a piece of a white shroud I had with me and tying it to a staff, ran along the seashore making signals therewith and calling to the people in the ship, until they espied me and hearing my shouts, sent a boat to fetch me off. When it drew near, the crew called out to me, saying, "Who art

thou and how camest thou to be on this mountain, whereon never saw we any in our born days?"

I answered, "I am a gentleman and a merchant who hath been wrecked and saved myself on one of the planks of the ship, with some of my goods."

So they took me in their boat, together with the bundles I had made of the jewels and valuables from the cavern, tied up in clothes and shrouds and rowed back with me to the ship, where the captain said to me, "How camest thou, O man, to yonder place on yonder mountain behind which lieth a great city? All my life I have sailed these seas and passed to and fro hard by these heights, yet never saw I here any living thing save wild beasts and birds." I repeated to him the story I had told the sailors, but acquainted him with nothing of that which had befallen me in the city and the cavern, lest there should be any of the islanders in the ship. Then I took out some of the best pearls I had with me and offered them to the captain. But he refused to accept it of me, saying, "When we find a shipwrecked man on the seashore or on an island, we take him up and give him meat and drink and if he be naked we clothe him, nor take we aught from him, when we reach a port of safety, we set him ashore with a present of our own money and entreat him kindly and charitably." So I prayed that his life be long in the land and rejoiced in my escape.

Then we pursued our voyage and sailed from island to island and sea to sea until at last by the decree of Allah we arrived in safety at Bassorah, where I tarried a few days, then went on to Baghdad and finding my quarter, entered my house with lively pleasure. There I forgathered with my family and friends, who rejoiced in my happy return and give me joy of my safety. I laid up in my storehouses all the goods I had brought with me and gave alms and largess to fakirs and beggars and clothed the widow and the orphan. Then I gave myself up to pleasure and enjoyment, returning to my old merry mode of rife. Such, then, be the most marvellous adventures of my fourth voyage, but tomorrow, if you will kindly come to me, I will tell you that which befell me in my fifth voyage, which was yet rarer and more marvellous than those which forewent it.

When Sindbad the Seaman had made an end of his story, he called for supper, so they spread the table and the guests ate the evening meal, after which he gave the porter a hundred dinars as usual and he and the rest of the company went their ways.

The Fifth Voyage of Sindbad the Seaman

Illustrated by Cecilia Carlstedt

Know, O my brothers, that when I had been awhile on shore after my fourth voyage and when, in my comfort and pleasures and in my rejoicing over my large gains and profits, I had forgotten all I had endured of perils and sufferings, the carnal man was again seized with the longing to travel and to see foreign countries and islands. Accordingly I bought costly merchandise suited to my purpose and, making it up into bales, repaired to Bassorah, where I walked about the river quay until I found a fine tall ship, newly built with gear unused and fitted ready for sea. She pleased me, so I bought her and, embarking my goods in her, hired a master and crew, over whom I set certain of my slaves and servants as inspectors. A number of merchants also brought their outfits and paid me freight and passage money. Then we set sail over Allah's pool in all joy and cheer, promising ourselves a prosperous voyage and much profit.

We sailed from city to city and from island to island and from sea to sea viewing the cities and countries by which we passed and selling and buying in not a few, until one day we came to a great uninhabited island, deserted and desolate, whereon was a white dome of biggest bulk half buried in the sands. The merchants landed to examine this dome, leaving me in the ship and when they drew near, behold, it was a huge roc's egg. They fell a-beating it with stones, knowing not what it was and presently broke it open, whereupon much water ran out of it and the young roc appeared within. So they pulled it forth of the shell and cut its throat and took of it a great store of meat.

Now I was in the ship and knew not what they did, but presently one of the passengers came up to me and said, "O my lord, come and look at the egg that we thought to be a dome."

So I looked and seeing the merchants beating it with stones, called out to them, "Stop, stop! Do not meddle with that egg, or the bird roc will come out and break our ship and destroy us." But they paid no heed to me and gave not over smiting upon the egg, when behold, the day grew dark and the sun was hidden from us, as if some great cloud had passed over the firmament. So we raised our eyes and saw that what we took for a cloud was the roc poised between us and the sun and it was his wings that darkened the day. When it came and saw its egg broken, it cried a loud cry, whereupon its mate came flying up and they both began circling about the ship, crying out at us with voices louder than thunder. I called to the Rais and crew, "Put out to sea and seek safety in flight, before we be all destroyed!" So the merchants came on board and we cast off and made haste from the island to gain the open sea. When the rocs saw this, they flew off and we crowded all sail on the ship, thinking to get out of their country, but presently the two reappeared and flew after us and stood over us, each carrying in its claws a huge boulder which it had brought from the mountains. As soon as the he-roc came up with us, he let fall upon us the rock he held in his pounces, but the master put about ship, so that the rock missed her by some small matter and plunged into the waves with such violence that the ship pitched high and then sank into the trough of the sea and the bottom the ocean appeared to us. Then the she-roc let fall her rock, which was bigger than that of her mate and as destiny had decreed, it fell on the poop of the ship and crushed it, the rudder flying into twenty pieces. Whereupon the vessel foundered and all and everything on board were cast into the sea. As for me, I struggled for sweet life until Almighty Allah threw in my way one of the planks of the ship, to which I clung and bestriding it, fell a-paddling with my feet.

Now the ship had gone down hard by an island in the midst of the main and the winds and waves bore me on until they cast me up on the shore of the island, at the last gasp for toil and distress and half-dead with hunger and thirst. So I landed more like a corpse than a live man and throwing myself down on the beach, lay there awhile until I began to revive and recover spirits, when I walked about the island and found it as it were one of the garths and gardens of Paradise. Its trees bore ripe yellow fruit for freight, its streams ran clear and bright, its flowers were fair to scent and to sight and its birds warbled with delight the praises of Him to whom belong permanence and all-might. So I ate my fill of the fruits and slaked my thirst with the water of the streams until I could no more and I returned thanks to Allah, after which I sat until nightfall hearing no voice and seeing none inhabitant. Then I lay down and slept without surcease until morning, when I arose and walked about under the trees until I came to the channel of a draw well fed by

a spring of running water, by which well sat an old man of venerable aspect, girt about with a waistcloth made of the fibre of palm fronds. Quoth I to myself, "Haply this Sheikh is of those who were wrecked in the ship and hath made his way to this island."

So I drew near to him and saluted him and he returned my salaam by signs, but spoke not and I said to him, "What causeth thee to sit here?" He shook his head and moaned and signed to me with his hand as who should say, "Take me on thy shoulders and carry me to the other side of the well channel."

And quoth I in my mind, "I will deal kindly with him and do what he desireth. It may be I shall win me a reward in Heaven, for he may be a paralytic."

So I took him on my back and carrying him to the place whereat he pointed, said to him, "Dismount at thy leisure." But he would not get off my back and wound his legs about my neck. I looked at them and seeing that they were like a buffalo's hide for blackness and roughness, was affrighted and would have cast him off, but he clung to me and gripped my neck with his legs until I was well-nigh choked. The world grew black in my sight and I fell senseless to the ground like one dead. But he kept his seat and raising his legs, drummed with his heels and beat harder than palm rods my back

and shoulders, until he forced me to rise for excess of pain. Then he signed to me with his hand to carry him hither and thither among the trees which bore the best fruits and if ever I refused to do his bidding or loitered or took my leisure, he beat me with his feet more grievously than if I had been beaten with whips. So I carried him about the island, like a captive slave and he dismounted not night or day. And whenas he wished to sleep, he wound his legs about my neck and leaned back and slept awhile, then arose and beat me, whereupon I sprang up in haste, unable to gainsay him because of the pain he inflicted on me. And indeed I blamed myself and sore repented me of having taken compassion on him and continued in this condition, suffering fatigue not to be described, until I said to myself, "I wrought him a weal and he requited me with my ill. By Allah, never more will I do any man a service so long as I live!"

And thus I abode a long while until one day I came with him to a place wherein was an abundance of gourds, many of them dry. So I took a great dry gourd and cutting open the head, scooped out the inside and cleaned it, after which I gathered grapes from a vine which grew hard by and squeezed them into the gourd until it was full of the juice. Then I stopped up the mouth and set it in the sun, where I left it for some days until it became strong wine and every day I used to drink of it, to comfort and sustain me under my fatigues with that obstinate fiend. And as often as I drank myself drunk, I forgot my troubles and took new heart.

One day he saw me and signed to me with his hand, as who should say, "What is that?" Quoth I, "It is an excellent cordial, which cheereth the heart and reviveth the spirits." Then, being heated with wine, I ran and danced with him among the trees, clapping my hands and singing and making merry and I staggered under him by design. When he saw this, he signed to me to give him the gourd that he might drink and I feared him and gave it him. So he took it and draining it to the dregs, cast it on the ground, whereupon he grew frolicsome and began to clap hands and jig to and fro on my shoulders. But presently, the fumes of the wine rising to his head, he became helplessly drunk and his side muscles and limbs relaxed and he swayed to and fro on my back. When I saw that he had lost his senses for drunkenness, I put my hand to his legs and, loosening them from my neck, stooped down well-nigh to the ground and threw him at full length. Then I took up a great stone from among the trees and coming up to him, smote him therewith on the head with all my might and killed him!

I then returned, with a heart at ease, to my former station on the seashore and abode in that island many days, eating of its fruits and drinking of its waters and keeping a look-out for passing ships, until one day, as I sat on the beach recalling all that had befallen me and saying, "I wonder if Allah will save me alive and restore me to my home and family and friends!", behold, a ship was making for the island through the dashing sea and clashing waves. Presently it cast anchor and the passengers landed, so I made for them and when they saw me all hastened up to me and gathering round me, questioned me of my case and how I came thither. I told them all that had betided me, whereat they marvelled with exceeding marvel and said, "He who rode on thy shoulder is called the Sheikh-al-Bahr or Old Man of the Sea and none ever felt his legs on neck and came off alive but thou and those who die under him he eateth. So praised be Allah for thy safety!" Then they set somewhat of food before me, whereof I ate my fill and gave me somewhat of clothes, wherewith I clad myself anew and covered my nakedness. After which they took me up into the ship and we sailed days and nights until fate brought us to a place called the City of Apes, built with lofty houses, all of which gave upon the sea and it had a single gate studded and strengthened with iron nails.

Now every night as soon as it is dusk the dwellers in this city used to come forth of the gates and, putting out to sea in boats and ships, pass the night upon the waters in their fear lest the apes should come down on them from the mountains. Hearing this, I was sore troubled, remembering what I had before suffered from the ape kind. Presently I landed to solace myself in the city, but meanwhile the ship set sail without me and I repented of having gone ashore and calling to mind my companions and what had befallen me with the apes, first and after, sat down and fell aweeping and lamenting. Presently one of the townsfolk accosted me and said to me, "O my lord, thou art a stranger to these parts?"

"Yes," answered I, "I am indeed a stranger and a poor one, who came hither in a ship which cast anchor here and I landed to visit the town. But when I would have gone on board again, I found they had sailed without me."

Quoth he, "Come and embark with us, for if thou lie the night in the city, the apes will destroy thee."

"Hearkening and obedience," replied I and rising, straightway embarked with him in one of the boats, whereupon they pushed off from shore and anchoring a mile or so from the land, there passed the night. At daybreak they rowed back to the city and landing, went each about his business. Thus they did every night, for if any tarried in the town

119

by night the apes came down on him and slew him. As soon as it was day, the apes left the place and ate of the fruits of the gardens, then went back to the mountains and slept there until nightfall, when they again came down upon the city. One night in the boat my company asked me, "O my lord, thou art apparently a stranger in these parts. Hast thou any craft whereat thou canst work?" and I answered, "By Allah, O my brother, I have no trade nor know I any handicraft, for I was a merchant and a man of money and substance and had a ship of my own, laden with great store of goods and merchandise. But it foundered at sea and all were drowned except me, who saved myself on a piece of plank which Allah vouchsafed to me of His favour."

Upon this he brought me a cotton bag and giving it to me, said, "Take this bag and fill it with pebbles from the beach and go forth with a company of the townsfolk to whom I will give a charge respecting thee. Do as they do and belike thou shalt gain what may further thy return voyage to thy native land." Then he carried me to the beach, where I filled my bag with pebbles large and small and presently we saw a company of people issue from the town, each bearing a bag like mine, filled with pebbles. To these he committed me, commending me to their care, saying, "This man is a stranger, so take him with you and teach him how to gather, so that he may get his daily bread and you will earn your reward and recompense in Heaven." "On our head and eyes be it!" answered they and bidding me welcome, fared on with me until we came to a spacious wady, full of lofty trees with trunks so smooth that none might climb them.

Now sleeping under these trees were many apes, which when they saw us rose and fled from us and swarmed up among the branches, whereupon my companions began to pelt them with what they had in their bags and the apes fell to plucking the fruit of the trees and casting them at the people. I looked at the fruits they cast at us and found them to be coconuts, so I chose a great tree full of apes and going up to it, began to pelt them with stones and they in return pelted me with nuts, which I collected, as did the rest. So that even before I had made an end of my bagful of pebbles, I had got great plenty of nuts. And as soon as my companions had in like manner got as many nuts as they could carry, we returned to the city, where we arrived at the end of day. Then I went in to the kindly man who had brought me in company with the nut-gatherers and gave him all I had got, thanking him for his kindness, but he would not accept them, saying, "Sell them and make profit by the price," and presently he added, giving me the key of a closet in his house, "Store thy nuts in this safe place and go thou forth every morning and gather them as thou hast done today and choose the worst for sale and supplying thyself, but lay up the rest here, so haply thou mayst collect enough to serve thee for thy return home."

"Allah requite thee!" answered I and did as he advised me, going out daily with the coco-nut gatherers, who commended me to one another and showed me the best-stocked trees. Thus did I for some time, until I had laid up great store of excellent nuts, besides a large sum of money, the price of those I had sold. I became thus at my ease and bought all I saw and had a mind to and passed my time pleasantly, greatly enjoying my stay in the city, until as I stood on the beach one day a great ship steering through the heart of the sea presently cast anchor by the shore and landed a company of merchants, who proceeded to sell and buy and barter their goods for coconuts and other commodities. Then I went to my friend and told him of the coming of the ship and how I had a mind to return to my own country, and he said, "It is for thee to decide."

So I thanked him for his bounties and took leave of him. Then, going to the captain of the ship, I agreed with him for my passage and embarked my coconuts and what else I possessed. We weighed anchor the same day and sailed from island to island and sea to sea and whenever we stopped, I sold and traded with my coconuts and the Lord

requited me more than I had had and lost. Amongst other places, we came to an island abounding in cloves and cinnamon and pepper and the country people told me that by the side of each pepper bunch groweth a great leaf which shadeth it from the sun and casteth the water off it in the wet season, but when the rain ceaseth, the leaf turneth over and droopeth down by the side of the bunch. Here I took in great store of pepper and cloves and cinnamon in exchange for coconuts and we passed thence to the Island of Al-Usirat, whence cometh the Comorin aloes wood and thence to another island, five days' journey in length, where grows the Chinese lign aloes, which is better than the Comorin. But the people of this island are fouler of condition and religion than those of the other, for that they love fornication and wine bibbing and know not prayer nor call to prayer. Thence we came to the pearl fisheries and I gave the divers some of my coconuts and said to them, "Dive for my luck and lot!" They did so and brought up from the deep bright great store of large and priceless pearls and they said to me, "By Allah, O my master, thy luck is a lucky!"

Then we sailed on, with the blessing of Allah and ceased not sailing until we arrived safely at Bassorah. There I abode a little and then went on to Baghdad, where I entered my quarter and found my house and forgathered with my family and saluted my friends, who gave me joy of my safe return and I laid up all my goods and valuables in my storehouses. Then I distributed alms and largess and clothed the widow and the orphan and made presents to my relations and comrades, for the Lord had requited me fourfold that I had lost. After which I returned to my old merry way of life and forgot all I had suffered in the great profit and gain I had made. Such, then, is the history of my fifth voyage and its wonderments and now to supper and tomorrow, come again and I will tell you what befell me in my sixth voyage, for it was even more wonderful than this.

Then he called for food and the servants spread the table and when they had eaten the evening meal, he bade to give Sindbad the Porter a hundred golden dinars and the landsman returned home and lay him down to sleep, much marvelling at all he had heard. Next morning, as soon as it was light, he prayed the dawn prayer and, after blessing Mohammed, betook himself to the house of Sindbad the Seaman and wished him a good day. The merchant bade to him sit and talked with him the rest of the company arrived. Then the servants spread the table and when they had well eaten and drunken and were mirthful and merry, Sindbad the Seaman began in these words the narrative of the Sixth Voyage of Sindbad the Seaman.

The Sixth Voyage of Sindbad the Seaman

Illustrated by Kate Sutton

Know, O my brothers and friends and companions all, that I abode some time, after my return from my fifth voyage, in great solace and satisfaction and mirth and merriment and enjoyment, and I forgot what I had suffered, seeing the great gain and profit I had made, until one day as I sat making merry and enjoying myself with my friends, there came in to me a company of merchants whose case told tales of travel and they talked with me of voyage and adventure and greatness of pelf and lucre. Hereupon I remembered the days of my return abroad and my joy at once more seeing my native land and forgathering with my family and friends and my soul yearned for travel and traffic.

So, compelled by fate and fortune, I resolved to undertake another voyage and, buying me fine and costly merchandise meet for foreign trade, made it up into bales, with which I journeyed from Baghdad to Bassorah. Here I found a great ship ready for sea and full of merchants and notables, who had with them goods of price, so I embarked my bales therein. And we left Bassorah in safety and good spirits under the safeguard of the King, the Preserver and continued our voyage from place to place and from city to city, buying and selling and profiting and diverting ourselves with the sight of countries where strange people dwell. And fortune and the voyage smiled upon us until one day, as we went along, behold, the captain suddenly cried with a great cry and cast his turban on the deck. Then he buffeted his face like a woman and plucked out his beard and fell down in the waist of the ship well-nigh fainting for stress of grief and rage and crying, "Oh and alas for the ruin of my house and the orphanship of my poor children!"

So all the merchants and sailors came round about him and asked him, "O master, what is the matter?"

And he answered, saying, "Know, O people, that we have wandered from our course and left the sea whose ways we know and come into a sea whose ways I know not and unless Allah vouchsafe us a means of escape, we are all dead men. Wherefore pray ye to the Most High that He deliver us from this strait. Haply amongst you is one righteous whose prayers the Lord will accept."

Then he arose and climbed the mast to see if there were any escape from that strait. And he would have loosed the sails, but the wind redoubled upon the ship and whirled her round thrice and drove her backward, whereupon her rudder broke and she fell off toward a high mountain. With this the captain came down from the mast, saying, "There is no Majesty and there is no Might save in Allah, the Glorious, the Great, nor can man prevent that which is foreordained of fate! By Allah, we are fallen on a place of sure destruction and there is no way of escape for us, nor can any of us be saved!"

Presently the ship struck the mountain and broke up and all and everything on board of her were plunged into the sea. Some of the merchants were drowned and others made shift to reach the shore and save themselves upon the mountain, I amongst their number. And when we got ashore, we found a great island, or rather peninsula. So I climbed the cliffs into the inward of the isle and walked on inland until I came to a stream of sweet water that welled up at the nearest foot of the mountains and disappeared in the earth under the range of hills on the opposite side. But all the other passengers went over the mountains to the inner tracts and, dispersing hither and thither, were confounded at what they saw and became like madmen at the sight of the wealth and treasures wherewith the shores were strewn. As for me, I looked into the bed of the stream aforesaid and saw therein great plenty of rubies and great royal pearls and all kinds of jewels and precious stones, which were as gravel in the bed of the rivulets that ran through the fields and the sands sparkled and glittered with gems and precious ores. We continued thus to explore the island, marvelling at the wonderful works of Allah and the riches we found there, but sore troubled for our own case and dismayed at our prospects.

Now we had picked up on the beach some small matter of victual from the wreck and husbanded it carefully eating but once every day or two, in our fear lest it should fail us and we die miserably of famine and affright. Moreover, we were weak for colic brought on by seasickness and low diet and my companions deceased, one after other, until I had buried the last of the party and abode alone on the island with but a little provision left. And I wept over myself, saying, "Would Heaven I had died before my companions

and they had washed me and buried me! It had been better than I should perish and none wash me and shroud me and bury me. But there is no Majesty and there is no Might save in Allah, the glorious, the Great!"

Now after I had buried the last of my party and abode alone on the island, I arose and dug me a deep grave on the seashore, saying to myself, "Whenas I grow weak and know that death cometh to me, I will cast myself into the grave and die there, so the wind may drift the sand over me and cover me and I be buried therein." Then I fell to reproaching myself for my little wit in leaving my native land and betaking me again to travel after all I had suffered during my first five voyages especially when I had not made a single one without suffering more horrible perils and more terrible hardships than in its forerunners and having no hope of escape from my present stress. However, after a while Allah sent me a thought and I said to myself, "By God, this stream must have an end as well as a beginning, its course may lead to some inhabited place. So my best plan is to make me a little boat big enough to sit in and carry it and, launching it on the river, embark therein and drop down the stream. If I escape, I escape, by God's leave and if I perish, better die in the river than here." Then, sighing for myself, I set to

work collecting a number of pieces of wood and I bound them together with ropes from the wreckage. Then I chose from the broken-up ships straight planks of even size and fixed them firmly upon the wood, making me a raft a little narrower than the channel of the stream and I tied it tightly and firmly as though it were nailed. Then I loaded it with the goods, precious ores and jewels and the union pearls which were like gravel and the best of the ambergris crude and pure, together with what I had collected on the island and what was left me of victual and wild herbs. Lastly I lashed a piece of wood on either side, to serve me as oars, and launched it.

My raft drifted with the stream, I pondered the issue of my affair and the drifting ceased not until I came to the place where it disappeared beneath the mountain. I rowed my conveyance into the place, which was intensely dark and the current carried the raft with it down the underground channel. The thin stream bore me on through a narrow tunnel where the raft touched either side and my head rubbed against the roof, return there from being impossible. Then I blamed myself for having thus risked my life and said, "If this passage grows any straighter, the raft will hardly pass and I cannot turn back, so I shall inevitably perish miserably in this place." And I threw myself down upon my face on the raft, by reason of the narrowness of the channel, whilst the stream ceased not to carry me along, knowing not night from day for the excess of the gloom which encompassed me and my terror and concern for myself lest I should perish. And in such condition my course continued down the channel, which now grew wider and then straighter.

Sore and weary by reason of the darkness which could be felt, I fell asleep as I lay prone on the craft and I slept knowing not if the time were long or short. When I awoke at last, I found myself in the light of Heaven and opening my eyes, I saw myself in a broad of the stream and the raft moored to an island in the midst of a number of Indians and Abyssinians. As soon as they saw that I was awake, they came up to me and bespoke me in their speech. But I understood not what they said and thought that this was a dream and a vision which had betided me for stress of concern and chagrin. But I was delighted at my escape from the river. When they saw I understood them not and made them no answer, one of them came forward and said to me in Arabic, "Peace be with thee, O my brother! Who art thou and whence faredst thou hither? How camest thou into this river and what manner of land lies behind yonder mountains, for never knew we anyone make his way thence to us?"

Quoth I, "And upon thee be peace! Who are ye and what country is this?"

"O my brother," answered he, "we are husbandmen and workers of the soil, who came out to water our fields and plantations and finding thee asleep on this raft, laid hold of it and made it fast by us, against thou shouldst awake at thy leisure. So tell us how thou camest hither."

I answered, "For Allah's sake, O my lord, ere I speak give me somewhat to eat, for I am starving and after ask me what thou wilt."

So he hastened to fetch me food and I ate my fill, until I was refreshed and my fear was calmed by a good bellyful and my life returned to me. Then I rendered thanks to Allah and told them all my adventures from first to last, especially my troubles in the narrow channel. They consulted among themselves and said to one another, "There is no help for it but we carry him with us and present him to our King, so that he may acquaint him with his adventures."

So they took me, together with my raft and its lading of moneys and merchandise, jewels, minerals and golden gear and brought me to their King, who was King of Sarandib, telling him what had happened. Whereupon he saluted me and bade me welcome. Then he questioned me of my condition and adventures through the man who had spoken Arabic and I repeated to him my story from beginning to end, whereat he marvelled exceedingly and gave me joy of my deliverance. After which I arose and fetched from the raft great store of precious ores and jewels and ambergris and lip aloes and presented them to the King, who accepted them and entreated me with the utmost honour, appointing me an abode in his own palace. So I consorted with the chief of the islanders and they paid me the utmost respect. And I quitted not the royal palace.

Now the Island Sarandib lieth under the equinoctial line, its night and day both numbering twelve hours. It measureth eighty leagues long by a breadth of thirty and its width is bounded by a lofty mountain and a deep valley. The surface is covered with emery, wherewith gems are cut and fashioned, diamonds are in its rivers and pearls are in its valleys. I ascended that mountain and solaced myself with a view of its marvels, which are indescribable and afterward I returned to the King. Thereupon all the travellers and merchants who came to the place questioned me of the affairs of my native land and of the Caliph Harun al-Rashid and his rule and I told them of him and of that wherefore he was renowned and they praised him because of this, whilst I in turn questioned them of the manners and customs of their own countries and got the knowledge I desired.

One day the King himself asked me of the fashions and form of government of my country and I acquainted him with the circumstance of the Caliph's sway in the city of Baghdad and the justice of his rule. The King marvelled at my account of his appointments and said, "By Allah, the Caliph's ordinances are indeed wise and his fashions of praiseworthy guise and thou hast made me love him by what thou tellest me. Wherefore I have a mind to make him a present and send it by thee."

Quoth I, "Hearkening and obedience, O my lord. I will bear thy gift to him and inform him that thou art his sincere admirer and true friend."

Then I abode with the King in great honour and regard and consideration for a long while until one day, as I sat in his palace, I heard news of a company of merchants that were fitting out ship for Bassorah and said to myself, "I cannot do better than voyage with these men." So I rose without stay or delay and kissed the King's hand and acquainted him with my longing to set out with the merchants, for that I pined after my people and mine own land.

Quoth he, "Thou art thine own master, yet if it be thy will to abide with us, on our head and eyes be it, for thou gladdenest us with thy company."

"By Allah, O my lord," answered I, "thou hast indeed overwhelmed me with thy favours and well-doings, but I weary for a sight of my friends and family and native country."

When he heard this, he summoned the merchants in question and commended me to their care, paying my freight and passage money. Then he bestowed on me great riches from his treasuries and charged me with a magnificent present for the Caliph Harun al-Rashid. Moreover, he gave me a sealed letter, saying, "Carry this with thine own hand to the Commander of the Faithful and give him many salutations from us!" The missive was written on the skin of the khawi with ink of ultramarine and the contents were as follows,

"Peace be with thee from the King of Al-Hind, before whom are a thousand elephants and upon whose palace crenelles are a thousand jewels. We send thee a trifling gift, which be thou pleased to accept. Thou art to us a brother and a sincere friend and great is the love we bear for thee in heart. Favour us therefore with a reply. The gift besitteth not thy dignity, but we beg of thee, O our brother, graciously to accept it and peace be with thee."

And the present was a cup of ruby a span high, the inside of which was adorned with precious pearls, and a bed covered with the skin of the serpent which swalloweth the

elephant, which skin hath spots each like a dinar, and a hundred thousand miskals of Indian lign aloes and a slave girl like a shining moon.

Then I took leave of him and of all my intimates and acquaintances on the island and embarked with the merchants aforesaid. We sailed with a fair wind, committing ourselves to the care of Allah and by His permission arrived at Bassorah, where I passed a few days and nights equipping myself and packing up my bales. Then I went on to Baghdad city, where I sought an audience of the Caliph and laid the King's presents before him. He asked me whence they came and I said to him, "By Allah, O Commander of the Faithful, I know not the name of the city nor the way thither!"

He then asked me, "O Sindbad, is this true which the King writeth?" and I answered, after kissing the ground,

"O my lord, I saw in his kingdom much more than he hath written in his letter. For state processions a throne is set for him upon a huge elephant eleven cubits high and upon this he sitteth having his great lords and officers and guests standing in two ranks, on his right hand and on his left. And when he mounteth horse there mount with him a thousand horsemen clad in gold brocade and silk. Moreover, by reason of his justice and ordinance and intelligence, there is no Kazi in his city and all his lieges distinguish between truth and falsehood."

Quoth the Caliph, "How great is this King! His letter hath shown me this and as for the mightiness of his dominion thou hast told us what thou hast eye-witnessed."

Then I related to the Commander of the Faithful all that had befallen me in my last voyage, at which he wondered exceedingly and bade his historians record my story and store it in his treasuries, for the edification of all who might see it. Then he conferred on me exceeding great favours and I repaired to my quarter and entered my home, where I warehoused all my goods and possessions. Presently my friends came to me and I distributed presents among my family and gave alms and largess, after which I yielded myself to enjoyment, mirth and merrymaking and forgot all that I had suffered. Such, then, O my brothers, is the history of what befell me in my sixth voyage and tomorrow, I will tell you the story of my seventh and last voyage, which is even more wondrous and marvellous than that of the first six.

The Seventh Voyage of Sindbad the Seaman

Illustrated by Mads Berg

Know, O company, that after my return from my sixth voyage, which brought me abundant profit, I resumed my former life in all possible joyance and enjoyment and mirth and making merry day and night. And I tarried sometime in this solace and satisfaction, until my soul began once more to long to sail the seas and see foreign countries and company with merchants and hear new things. So I packed up in bales a quantity of precious stuffs suited for sea trade and repaired with them from Baghdad to Bassorah, where I found a ship ready for sea and in her a company of considerable merchants. I shipped with them and, becoming friends, we set forth on our venture in health and safety and sailed with a wind until we came to a city called Madinat-al-Sin. But after we had left it, as we fared on in all cheer and confidence, behold, there sprang up a violent head wind and a tempest of rain fell on us and drenched us and our goods. So we covered the bales with our cloaks and garments and drugget and canvas, lest they be spoiled by the rain and betook ourselves to prayer and supplication to Almighty Allah and humbled ourselves before Him for deliverance from the peril that was upon us. But the captain arose and, tightening his girdle, tucked up his skirts and climbed to the masthead, whence he looked out right and left and gazing at the passengers and crew, fell to buffeting his face and plucking out his beard. So we cried to him, "O Rais, what is the matter?" and he replied, saying, "Seek ye deliverance of the Most High from the strait into which we have fallen and bemoan yourselves and take leave of one another. For know that the wind hath got the mastery of us and hath driven us into the uttermost of the sea's world."

Then he came down from the masthead and opening his sea chest, pulled but a bag of blue cotton, from which he took a powder like ash. This he set in a saucer wetted with a little water and after waiting a short time, smelt and tasted it. And then he took out

of the chest a booklet, wherein he read awhile and said, weeping, "Know, O ye passengers, that in this book is a marvellous matter, denoting that whoso cometh hither shall surely die. For that this ocean is called the Sea of the Clime of the King, wherein are serpents of vast bulk and fearsome aspect. And a great fish riseth and swalloweth what ship soever cometh to these climes."

Hearing these words from the captain, great was our wonder, but hardly had he made an end of speaking when the ship was lifted out of the water and let fall again and we applied to praying the death prayer and committing our souls to Allah. Presently we heard a terrible great cry like the loud-pealing thunder whereat we were terror-struck and became as dead men, giving ourselves up for lost. Then, behold, there came up to us a huge fish, as big as a tall mountain. Then suddenly a second fish made its appearance, than which we had seen naught more monstrous. So we bemoaned ourselves of our lives and farewelled one another. But suddenly up came a third fish bigger than the first two, whereupon we lost the power of thought and reason and were stupefied for the excess of our fear and horror. Then the three fish began circling round about the ship and the third and biggest opened its mouth to swallow it and we looked into its mouth and, behold, it was wider than the gate of a city and its throat was like a long valley. So

136

we besought the Almighty, when suddenly a violent squall of wind arose and smote the ship, which rose out of the water and settled upon a great reef where it broke up and fell asunder into planks and all and everything on board were plunged into the sea. As for me, I swam a little way, until I happened upon one of the ship's planks, whereto I clung and bestrode it like a horse. I was in the most piteous plight for fear and distress and hunger and thirst. And thus I abode for two days, at the end of which time I came to a great island abounding in trees and streams. There I landed and ate of the fruits of the island and drank of its waters, until I was refreshed and my life returned to me and my strength and spirits were restored. Then I walked about until I found on the further side a great river of sweet water, running with a strong current, whereupon I called to mind the raft I had made aforetime and said to myself, "Needs must I make another. Haply I may free me from this strait. If I escape, I have my desire and I vow to Allah Almighty to foreswear travel. And if I perish, I shall be at peace and shall rest from toil and moil."

So I rose up and gathered together great store of pieces of wood from the trees which were all of the finest sandalwood, and made shift to twist creepers and tree twigs into a kind of rope, with which I bound the billets together and so contrived a raft. Then saying, "If I be saved, 'tis of God's grace," I embarked thereon and committed myself to the current and it bore me on for the first day and the second and the third after leaving the island whilst I lay on the raft, eating not and drinking, when I was athirst, of the water of the river, until I was weak and giddy as a chicken for stress of fatigue and famine and fear. At the end of this time I came to a high mountain, whereunder ran the river, and I feared for my life by reason of the straitness I had suffered in my former journey, and I would fain have stayed the raft and landed on the mountainside. But the current overpowered me and drew it into the subterranean passage like an archway, whereupon I gave myself up for lost. However, after a little the raft glided into open air and I saw before me a wide valley, whereinto the river fell with a noise like the rolling of thunder and a swiftness as the rushing of the wind. I held onto the raft for fear of falling off it whilst the waves tossed me right and left and the craft continued to descend with the current.

Eventually it arrived at a great and goodly city, grandly edified and containing many people. And when the townsfolk saw me on the raft, dropping down with the current, they threw me out ropes, which I had not strength enough to hold. Then they tossed a net over the craft and drew it ashore, whereupon I fell to the ground amidst them, as

I were a dead man, for stress of fear and hunger and lack of sleep. After a while, there came up to me out of the crowd an old man of reverend aspect who welcomed me and threw over me abundance of handsome clothes, wherewith I covered my nakedness. Then he carried me to the hammam bath and brought me cordial sherbets and delicious perfumes. Moreover, when I came out, he bore me to his house, where his people set rich food before me, whereof I ate my fill and returned thanks to God the Most High for my deliverance. Also the Sheikh set apart for me an apartment in a part of his house and charged his pages and slave girls to wait upon me and do my will and supply my wants. They were assiduous in my service and I abode with him in the guest chamber for three days, taking my ease of good eating and good drinking and good scents until life returned to me. On the fourth day the Sheikh, my host, came in to me and said, "Thou cheerest us with thy company, O my son and praised be Allah for thy safety! Say, wilt thou now come down with me to the beach and the bazaar and sell thy goods and take their price? I ordered my servants to remove thy stock in trade from the sea and they have piled it on the shore."

I was silent awhile and said to myself, "What mean these words and what goods have I?" Then said he, "O my son, be not troubled nor careful, but come with me to the market and if any offer for thy goods contenteth thee, take it. But if thou be not satisfied, I will lay them up for thee in my warehouse, against a fitting occasion for sale."

So I bethought me of my case and said to myself, "Do his bidding and see what are these goods!" and I said to him, "O Sheikh I hear and obey. I may not gainsay thee in aught, for Allah's blessing is on all thou dost."

Accordingly he guided me to the market street, where I found that he had taken in pieces the raft which had carried me and which was of sandalwood and I heard the broker crying it for sale. Then the merchants came and opened the gate of bidding for the wood and bid against one another until its price reached a thousand dinars, when they left bidding and my host said to me, "Hear, O my son, this is the current price of thy goods in hard times like these. Wilt thou sell them for this, or shall I lay them up for thee in my storehouses until such time as prices rise?"

"O my lord," answered I, "the business is in thy hands. Do as thou wilt."

Then asked he, "Wilt thou sell the wood to me for a hundred gold pieces over and above what the merchants have bidden for it?" and I answered, "Yes, I have sold it to thee for monies received."

So he bade his servants to transport the wood to his storehouses, and, carrying me back to his house, seated me and counted out to me the purchase money. Some days after this the Sheikh said to me, "O my son, I have somewhat to propose to thee, wherein I trust thou wilt do my bidding."

Quoth I, "What is it?"

Quoth he, "I am a very old man and have no son, but I have a daughter who is young in years and fair of favour and endowed with abounding wealth and beauty. Now I have a mind to marry her to thee, that thou mayest abide with her in this our country. And I will make thee master of all I have in hand, for I am an old man and thou shalt stand in my stead."

I was silent for shame and made him no answer, whereupon he continued, "Do my desire in this, O my son, for I wish but thy weal. And if thou wilt but as I say, thou shalt have her at once and be as my son and all that is under my hand or that cometh to me shall be thine. If thou have a mind to traffic and travel to thy native land, none shall hinder thee and thy property will be at thy sole disposal. So do as thou wilt."

"By Allah, O my uncle," replied I, "thou art become to me even as my father and I am

140

a stranger and have undergone many hardships, while for stress of that which I have suffered naught of judgment or knowledge is left to me. It is for thee, therefore, to decide what I shall do." Hereupon he sent his servants for the Kazi and the witnesses and married me to his daughter. When I went in to her, I found her perfect in beauty and loveliness. She pleased me and we loved each other and I abode with her in all solace and delight of life until her father was taken to the mercy of Allah Almighty. So we shrouded him and buried him and I laid hands on the whole of his property and all his servants and slaves became mine. Moreover, the merchants installed me in his office, for he was their Sheikh and their chief and none of them purchased aught but with his knowledge and by his leave.

When I became acquainted with the townsfolk, I found that at the beginning of each month they were transformed, in that their faces changed and they became like unto birds and they put forth wings wherewith they flew unto the upper regions of the firmament, and none remained in the city save the women and children. And I said in my mind, "When the first of the month cometh, I will ask one of them to carry me with them, whither they go." So when the time came and their complexion changed and their forms altered, I went in to one of the townsfolk and said to him, "Allah upon thee! Carry me with thee that I might divert myself with the rest and return with you."

"This may not be," answered he.

But I ceased not to solicit him and I importuned him until he consented. Then I went out in his company, without telling any of my family or servants or friends and he took me on his back and flew up with me so high in the air that I heard the angels glorifying God in the heavenly dome, whereat I wondered and exclaimed, "Praised be Allah! Hardly had I made an end of pronouncing the tasbih - praised be Allah! - when there came out a fire from Heaven and all but consumed the company. Whereupon they fled from it and descended with curses upon me and, casting me down on a high mountain, went away exceeding wroth with me and left me there alone. As I found myself in this plight, I repented of what I had done and reproached myself for having undertaken that for which I was unable, saying, "There is no Majesty and there is no Might save in Allah, the Glorious, the Great! No sooner am I delivered from one affliction than I fall into a worse."

And I continued in this case, knowing not whither I should go, when suddenly there came up two young men, as they were moons, each using as a staff a rod of red gold.

So I approached and saluted them, and when they returned my salaam, I said to them, "Allah upon you twain. Who are ye and what are ye?"

Quoth they, "We are of the servants of the Most High Allah, abiding in this mountain," and giving me a rod of red gold they had with them, went their ways and left me. I walked on along the mountain ridge, staying my steps with the staff and pondering the case of the two youths, when behold, a serpent came forth from under the mountain with a man in its jaws whom it had swallowed even to below his navel and he was crying out and saying "Whoso delivereth me, Allah will deliver him from all adversity!"

So I went up to the serpent and smote it on the head with the golden staff, whereupon it cast the man forth of its mouth. Then I smote it a second time and it turned and fled, whereupon he came up to me and said, "Since my deliverance from yonder serpent hath been at thy hands I will never leave thee and thou shalt be my comrade on this mountain."

"And welcome," answered I. So we fared on along the mountain until we fell in with a company of people and I looked and saw amongst them the very man who had carried me and cast me down there. I went up to him and spake him fair, excusing to him and saying, "O my comrade, it is not thus that friend should deal with friend."

Quoth he, "It was thou who well-nigh destroyed us by thy tasbih and thy glorifying God on my back."

Quoth I, "Pardon me, for I had no knowledge of this matter, but if thou wilt take me with thee, I swear not to say a word."

So he relented and consented to carry me with him, but he made an express condition that so long as I abode on his back, I should abstain from pronouncing the tasbih or otherwise glorifying God. Then I gave the wand of gold to him whom I had delivered from the serpent and bade him farewell and my friend took me on his back and flew with me as before, until he brought me to the city and set me down in my own house. My wife came to meet me and, saluting me, gave me joy of my safety and then said, "Beware of going forth hereafter with yonder folk, neither consort with them, for they are brethren of the devils and know not how to mention the name of Allah Almighty. neither worship they Him."

"And how did thy father with them?" asked I, and she answered, "My father was not of them, neither did he as they. And as now he is dead, methinks thou hadst better sell all we have and journey to thine own country and people and I with thee."

So I sold all my property and looked for one who should be journeying to Bassorah. And while thus doing I heard of a company of townsfolk who had a mind to make the voyage so we embarked, I and my wife, with all our movables and ceased not sailing until we arrived at Bassorah. I made no stay there, but freighted another vessel and, transferring my goods to her, set out for Baghdad, where I arrived in safety and entering my quarter and repairing to my house, forgathered with my family and friends and familiars and laid up my goods in my warehouses. When my people, who, reckoning the period of my absence on this my seventh voyage, had found it to be seven and twenty years and had given up all hope of me, heard of my return, they came to welcome me and to give me joy of my safety. And I related to them all that had befallen me, whereat they marvelled with exceeding marvel. Then I foreswore travel and vowed to Allah the Most High I would venture no more by land or sea.

"Consider, therefore, O Sindbad, O Landsman," continued Sindbad the Seaman, "what sufferings I have undergone and what perils and hardships I have endured before coming to my present state."

"Allah upon thee, O my Lord!" answered Sindbad the Landsman. "Pardon me the wrong I did thee." And they ceased not from friendship and fellowship, abiding in all cheer and pleasures and solace of life.

The Third Kalandar's Tale

Illustrated by Pipa

My name is Ajib, the son of Khazib, who reigned over a large kingdom, which had for its capital one of the finest seaport towns in the world. When my father died I succeeded him and I ruled and did justice and dealt fairly by all my lieges. I delighted in sea trips, for my capital stood on the shore, before which the ocean stretched far and wide and near hand were many great islands with sconces and garrisons in the midst of the main. My fleet numbered fifty merchantmen and as many yachts for pleasance and a hundred and fifty sail ready fitted for holy war with the unbelievers.

It fortuned that I had a mind to enjoy myself on the islands aforesaid, so I took ship with my people in ten keel and, carrying with me a month's victual, I set out on a twenty days' voyage.

But one night a head wind struck us and the sea rose against us with huge waves. The billows sorely buffeted us and a dense darkness settled round us. We gave ourselves up for lost and I said, "Whoso endangereth his days, deserveth no praise." Then we prayed to Allah and besought Him, but the storm blasts ceased not to blow against us nor the surges to strike us until morning broke, when the gale fell, the seas sank to mirrory stillness and the sun shone upon us kindly clear. Presently we made to an island, where we landed and cooked somewhat of food and ate heartily and took our rest for a couple of days. Then we set out again and sailed other twenty days, the seas broadening and the land shrinking.

Presently the current ran counter to us and we found ourselves in strange waters, where the Captain had lost his reckoning and was wholly bewildered in this sea, so said we to the lookout man, "Get thee to the masthead and keep thine eyes open."

He swarmed up the mast and looked out and cried aloud, "O Rais, I espy to starboard

something dark, very like a fish floating on the face of the sea and to larboard there is a loom in the midst of the main, now black and now bright."

When the Captain heard the lookout's words, he dashed his turban on the deck and plucked out his beard and beat his face, saying, "Good news indeed! We be all dead men, not one of us can be saved." And he fell to weeping and all of us wept for his weeping and also for our lives and I said, "O Captain, tell us what it is the lookout saw."

"O my Prince," answered he, "know that we lost our course on the night of the storm, which was followed on the morrow by a two days' calm during which we made no way and we have gone astray eleven days' reckoning from that night, with never a wind to bring us back to our true course. Tomorrow by the end of the day we shall come to a mountain of black stone, the Magnet Mountain, for thither the currents carry us willy-nilly. As soon as we are under its lea, the ship's sides will open and every nail in the planks will fly out and cleave fast to the mountain, for that Almighty Allah hath gifted the loadstone with a mysterious virtue and a love for iron, by reason whereof all which is iron travelleth toward it. And on this mountain is much iron, how much none knoweth save the Most High, from the many vessels which have been lost there since the days of yore. The bright spot upon its summit is a dome of yellow laton from Andalusia, vaulted upon ten columns. And on its crown is a horseman who rideth a horse of brass and holdeth in hand a lance of laton and there hangeth on his bosom a tablet of lead graven with names and talismans."

And he presently added, "And, O King, none destroyeth people save the rider on that steed, nor will the egromancy be dispelled until he falls from his horse."

Then the Captain wept with exceeding weeping and we all made sure of death doom and each and every one of us farewelled his friend and charged him with his last will and testament in case he might be saved. We slept not that night and in the morning we found ourselves much nearer the Loadstone Mountain, whither the waters drove us with a violent send.

When the ships were close under its lea, they opened and the nails flew out and all the iron in them sought the Magnet Mountain and clove to it like a network, so that by the end of the day we were all struggling in the waves round about the mountain. Some of us were saved, but more were drowned and even those who had escaped knew not one another, so stupefied were they by the beating of the billows and the raving of the winds. As for me, Allah preserved my life that I might suffer whatso He willed to me of hardship, misfortune and calamity, for I scrambled upon a plank from one of the ships and the wind and waters threw it at the feet of the mountain. There I found a practicable path leading by steps carven out of the rock to the summit and I called on the name of Allah Almighty and breasted the ascent, clinging to the steps and notches hewn in the stone and mounted little by little. And the Lord stilled the wind and aided me in the ascent, so that I succeeded in reaching the summit. There I found no resting place save the dome, which I entered, joying with exceeding joy at my escape and made the Wuzu ablution and prayed a two-bow prayer, a thanksgiving to God for my preservation.

Then I fell asleep under the dome and heard in my dream a mysterious voice saying, "O son of Khazib! When thou wakest from thy sleep, dig under thy feet and thou shalt find a bow of brass and three leaden arrows inscribed with talismans and characters. Take the bow and shoot the arrows at the horseman on the dome top and free mankind from this sore calamity. When thou hast shot him he shall fall into the sea and the horse will also drop at thy feet. Then bury it in the place of the bow. This done, the main will swell and rise until it is level with the mountain head and there will appear on it a skiff carrying a man of laton holding in his hand a pair of paddles. He will come to thee and do thou embark with him, but beware of saying Bismillah or of otherwise naming Allah Almighty. He will row thee for a space of ten days, until he bring thee to certain islands called the Islands of Safety and thence thou shalt easily reach a port and find those who will convey thee to thy native land. And all this shall be fulfilled to thee so thou call not on the name of Allah."

Then I started up from my sleep in joy and gladness and, hastening to do the bidding of the mysterious voice, found the bow and arrows and shot at the horseman and tumbled him into the main, whilst the horse dropped at my feet, so I took it and buried it. Presently the sea surged up and rose until it reached the top of the mountain, nor had I long to wait ere I saw a skiff in the offing coming toward me. I gave thanks to Allah and when the skiff came up to me, I saw therein a man of brass with a tablet of lead on his breast inscribed with talismans and characters and I embarked without uttering a word. The boatman rowed on with me through the first day and the second and the third, in all ten whole days, until I caught sight of the Islands of Safety, whereat I joyed with exceeding joy and for stress of gladness exclaimed, "Allah! Allah! In the name of Allah! There is no god but the God and Allah is Almighty."

Thereupon the skiff forthwith upset and cast me upon the sea, then it righted and sank deep into the depths.

Now I am a fair swimmer, so I swam the whole day until nightfall, when my forearms and shoulders were numbed with fatigue and I felt like to die, so I testified to my faith, expecting naught but death. The sea was still surging under the violence of the winds and presently there came a billow like a hillock and, bearing me up high in air, threw me with a long cast on dry land, that His will might be fulfilled.

I crawled upon the beach and doffing my raiment, wrung it out to dry and spread it in the sunshine. Then I lay me down and slept the whole night.

As soon as it was day, I donned my clothes and rose to look whither I should walk. Presently I came to a thicket of low trees and, making a cast round it, found that the spot whereon I stood was an islet, a mere holm, girt on all sides by the ocean, whereupon I said to myself, 'Whatso freeth me from one great calamity casteth me into a greater!"

But while I was pondering my case and longing for death, behold, I saw afar off a ship making for the island, so I climbed a tree and hid myself among the branches. Presently the ship anchored and landed ten slaves bearing iron hoes and baskets, who walked on

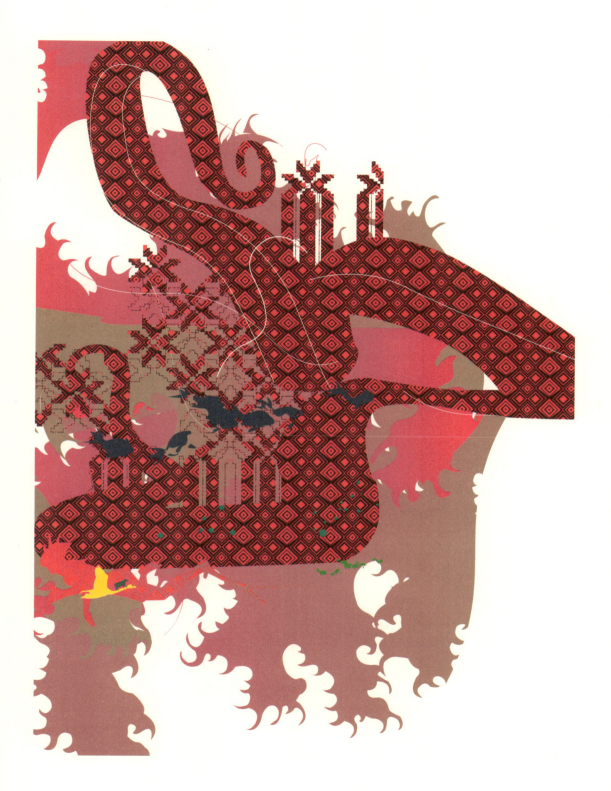

151

until they reached the middle of the island. Here they dug deep into the ground until they uncovered a plate of metal, which they lifted, thereby opening a trapdoor.

After this they returned to the ship and thence brought bread and flour, honey and fruits, clarified butter, leather bottles containing liquors and many household stuffs, also furniture, table service and mirrors, rugs, carpets and in fact all that is needed to furnish a dwelling. And they kept going to and fro, descending by the trapdoor, until they had transported into the dwelling all that was in the ship. After this the slaves again went on board and brought back with them garments as rich as may be and in the midst of them came an old man, of whom very little was left, for time had dealt hardly and harshly with him and all that remained of him was a bone wrapped in a rag of blue stuff, through which the winds whistled west and east. As saith the poet of him, "Time gars me tremble. Ah, how sore the balk! While time in pride of strength doth ever stalk. Time was I walked nor ever felt I tired, now am I tired albe' I never walk!" And the Sheikh held by the hand a youth cast in beauty's mould, all elegance and perfect grace, so fair that his comeliness deserved to be proverbial, for he was as a green bough or the tender young of the roe, ravishing every heart with his loveliness and subduing every soul with his coquetry and amorous ways. They stinted not their going until all went down by the trapdoor and did not reappear for an hour, or rather more, at the end of which time the slaves and the old man came up without the youth and, replacing the iron plate and carefully closing the door slab as it was before, they returned to the ship and made sail and were lost to my sight.

When they turned away to depart, I came down from the tree and, going to the place I had seen them fin up, scraped off and removed the earth and in patience possessed my soul until I had cleared the whole of it away. Then appeared the trapdoor, which was of wood, in shape and size like a millstone and when I lifted it up, it disclosed a winding staircase of stone. At this I marvelled and, descending the steps tier I reached the last, found a fair hall, spread with various kinds of carpets and silk stuffs, wherein was a youth sitting upon a raised couch and leaning back on a round cushion with a fan in his hand and nosegays and posies of sweet scented herbs and flowers before him. But he was alone and not a soul near him in the great vault. When he saw me he turned pale, but I saluted him courteously and said, "Set thy mind at ease and calm thy fears. No harm shall come near thee. I am a man like thyself and the son of a king to boot, whom the decrees of destiny have sent to bear thee company and cheer thee in

152

thy loneliness. But now tell me, what is thy story and what causeth thee to dwell thus in solitude under the ground?"

When he was assured that I was of his kind and no Jinni, he rejoiced and his fine colour returned and, making me draw near to him, he said, "O my brother, my story is a strange story and 'tis this. My father is a merchant jeweller possessed of great wealth, who hath white and black slaves travelling and trading on his account in ships and on camels and trafficking with the most distant cities, but he was not blessed with a child, not even one. Now on a certain night he dreamt a dream that he should be favoured with a son, who would be short-lived, so the morning dawned on my father, bringing him woe and weeping. On the following night my mother conceived and my father noted down the date of her becoming pregnant. Her time being fulfilled, she bare me, whereat my father rejoiced and made banquets and called together the neighbours and fed the fakirs and the poor, for that he had been blessed with issue near the end of his days. Then he assembled the astrologers and astronomers, who knew the places of the planets and the wizards and wise ones of the time and men learned in horoscopes and nativities and they drew out my birth scheme and said to my father, 'Thy son shall live

154

to fifteen years, but in his fifteenth there is a sinister aspect. If he safely tide it over, he shall attain a great age. And the cause that threateneth him with death is this. In the Sea of Peril standeth the Mountain Magnet, on whose summit is a horseman of yellow laton seated on a horse also of brass and bearing on his breast a tablet of lead. Fifty days after this rider shall fall from his steed thy son will die and his slayer will be he who shoots down the horseman, a Prince named Ajib son of King Khazib.' My father grieved with exceeding grief to hear these words, but reared me in tenderest fashion and educated me excellently well until my fifteenth year was told. Ten days ago news came to him that the horseman had fallen into the sea and he who shot him down was named Ajib son of King Khazib. My father thereupon wept bitter tears at the need of parting with me and became like one possessed of a Jinni. However, being in mortal fear for me, he built me this place under the earth and stocking it with all required for the few days still remaining, he brought me hither in a ship and left me here. Ten are already past and when the forty shall have gone by without danger to me, he will come and take me away, for he hath done all this only in fear of Prince Ajib. Such, then, is my story and the cause of my loneliness."

When I heard his history I marvelled and said in my mind, "I am the Prince Ajib who hath done all this, but as Allah is with me I will surely not slay him!"

So said I to him, "O my lord, far from thee be this hurt and harm and then, please Allah, thou shalt not suffer cark nor care nor aught disquietude, for I will tarry with thee and serve thee as a servant and then wend my ways. And after having borne thee company during the forty days, I will go with thee to thy home, where thou shalt give me an escort of some of thy Mamelukes with whom I may journey back to my own city and the Almighty shall requite thee for me."

He was glad to hear these words, when I rose and lighted a large wax candle and trimmed the lamps and the three lanterns and I set on meat and drink and sweet-meats. We ate and drank and sat talking over various matters until the greater part of the night was gone, when he lay down to rest and I covered him up and went to sleep myself.

Next morning I arose and warmed a little water, then lifted him gently so as to awake him and brought him the warm water, wherewith he washed his face and said to me, "Heaven requite thee for me with every blessing, O youth! By Allah, if I get quit of this danger and am saved from him whose name is Ajib bin Khazib, I will make my father

reward thee and send thee home healthy and wealthy. And if I die, then my blessing be upon thee."

I answered, "May the day never dawn on which evil shall betide thee and may Allah make my last day before thy last day!"

Then I set before him somewhat of food and we ate and I got ready perfumes for fumigating the hall, wherewith he was pleased. Moreover, I made him a mankalah cloth, and we played and ate sweetmeats and we played again and took our pleasure until nightfall, when I rose and lighted the lamps and set before him somewhat to eat and sat telling him stories until the hours of darkness were far spent.

Then he lay down to rest and I covered him up and rested also. And thus I continued to do for days and nights and affection for him took root in my heart and my sorrow was eased and I said to myself, "The astrologers lied when they predicted that he should be slain by Ajib bin Khazib. By Allah, I will not slay him."

I ceased not ministering to him and conversing and carousing with him and telling him all manner of tales for thirty-nine days. On the fortieth night the youth rejoiced and said, "O my brother, Alhamdolillah! Praise be to Allah, who hath preserved me from death and this is by thy blessing and the blessing of thy coming to me and I prayed God that He restore thee to thy native land. But now, O my brother, I would thou warm me some water for the ghusl ablution and do thou kindly bathe me and change my clothes."

I replied, "With love and gladness," and I heated water in plenty and carrying it in to him, washed his body all over, the washing of health, with meal of lupins and rubbed him well and changed his clothes and spread him a high bed whereon he lay down to rest, being drowsy after bathing.

Then said he, "O my brother, cut me up a watermelon and sweeten it with a little sugar candy." So I went to the storeroom and bringing out a fine watermelon, I found there, set it on a platter and laid it before him saying, "O my master, hast thou not a knife?" "Here it is," answered he, "over my head upon the high shelf."

So I got up in haste and, taking the knife, drew it from its sheath, but my foot slipped in stepping down and I fell heavily upon the youth holding in my hand the knife, which hastened to fulfil what had been written on the day that decided the destinies of man and it buried itself, as if planted, in the youth's heart. He died on the instant.

When I saw that he was slain and knew that I had slain him, mauger myself I cried out with an exceeding loud and bitter cry and beat my face and rent my raiment and said, "Verily we be Allah's and unto Him we be returning, O Moslems! O people fain of Allah! There remained for this youth but one day of the forty dangerous days which the astrologers and the learned had foretold for him and the predestined death of this beautiful one was to be at my hand. Would Heaven I had not tried to cut the watermelon! What dire misfortune is this I must bear, lief or loath? What a disaster! What an affliction! O Allah mine, I implore thy pardon and declare to Thee my innocence of his death. But what God willeth, let that come to pass."

When I was certified that I had slain him, I arose and, ascending the stairs, replaced the trapdoor and covered it with earth as before.

Then I looked out seaward and saw the ship cleaving the waters and making for the island, wherefore I was afeard and said, "The moment they come and see the youth done to death, they will know 'twas I who slew him and will slay me without respite." So I climbed up into a high tree and concealed myself among its leaves and hardly had I done so when the ship anchored and the slaves landed with the ancient man, the youth's father, and made direct for the place, and when they removed the earth they were surprised to see it soft.

Then they raised the trapdoor and went down and found the youth lying at full length, clothed in fair new garments, with a face beaming after the bath and the knife deep in his heart. At the sight they shrieked and wept and beat their faces, loudly cursing the murderer, whilst a swoon came over the Sheikh so that the slaves deemed him dead, unable to survive his son.

At last they wrapped the slain youth in his clothes and carried him up and laid him on the ground, covering him with a shroud of silk. Whilst they were making for the ship the old man revived and, gazing on his son who was stretched out, fell on the ground and strewed dust over his head and smote his face and plucked out his beard and his weeping redoubled as he thought of his murdered son and he swooned away once more.

After a while a slave went and fetched a strip of silk whereupon they lay the old man and sat down at his head. All this took place and I was on the tree above them watching everything that came to pass and my heart became hoary before my head waxed grey, for the hard lot which was mine and for the distress and anguish I had undergone and I fell to reciting, 'How many a joy by Allah's will hath fled with flight escaping sight of wisest head!

How many a sadness shall begin the day, yet grow right gladsome ere the day is sped! How many a weal trips on the heels of ill, causing the mourner's heart with joy to thrill!"

But the old man ceased not from his swoon until near sunset, when he came to himself and, looking upon his dead son, he recalled what had happened and how what he had dreaded had come to pass and he beat his face and head and recited these couplets, 'Racked is my heart by parting from my friends, and two rills ever from my eyelids flow. With them went forth my hopes, ah, well away! What shift remaineth me to say or do? Would I had never looked upon their sight, what shift, fair sirs, when paths ever strainer grow? What charm shall calm my pangs when this wise burn longings of love which in my vitals glow? Would I had trod with them the road of Death! Never had befell us twain this parting blow. Allah, I pray the truthful show me Roth and mix our lives nor part them evermore! How blest were we as 'death one roof we dwelt. Conjoined in joys nor recking aught of woe, until fortune shot us pith the severance shaft, ah who shall patient bear such parting throe? And dart of death struck down amid the tribe. The age's pearl that morn saw brightest show. I cried the while his case took speech and said, would Heaven, my son, death mote his doom foreslow! Which be the readiest road with

159

thee to meet my Son! For whom I would my soul bestow? If sun I call him no! The sun cloth set, if moon I call him, wane the moons, ah no! O sad mischance o' thee, O doom of days, thy place none other love shall ever know. Thy sire distracted sees thee, but despairs by wit or wisdom fate to overthrow. Some evil eye this day hath cast its spell and foul befall him as it foul betel!"

Then he sobbed a single sob and his soul fled his flesh. The slaves shrieked aloud, "Alas, our lord!" and showered dust on their heads and redoubled their weeping and wailing. Presently they carried their dead master to the ship side by side with his dead son and, having transported all the stuff from the dwelling to the vessel, set sail and disappeared from mine eyes. I descended from the tree and, raising the trapdoor, went down into the underground dwelling, where everything reminded me of the youth and I looked upon the poor remains of him and began repeating these verses, "Their tracks I see and pine with pain and pang, and on deserted hearths I weep and yearn. And Him I pray who doomed them depart some day vouchsafe the boon of safe return."

Then I went up again by the trapdoor and every day I used to wander round about the island and every night I returned to the underground hall. Thus I lived for a month, until at last, looking at the western side of the island, I observed that every day the tide ebbed, leaving shallow water for which the flow did not compensate and by the end of the month the sea showed dry land in that direction. At this I rejoiced, making certain of my safety, so I arose and, fording what little was left of the water, got me to the mainland, where I fell in with great heaps of loose sand in which even a camel's hoof would sink up to the knee. However, I emboldened my soul and, wading through the sand, saw a fire from afar burning with a blazing light. So I made for it hoping haply to find succour and broke out into these verses, "Belike my fortune may her bridle turn and time bring weal although he's jealous hight, forward my hopes and further all my needs, and passed ills with present weals requite."

And when I drew near the fire aforesaid, it was a palace with gates of copper burnished red which, when the rising sun shone thereon, gleamed and glistened from afar, showing what had seemed to me a fire. I rejoiced in the sight and sat down over against the gate, but I was hardly settled in my seat before there met me ten young men clothed in sumptuous gear and all were blind of the left eye, which appeared as plucked out. They were accompanied by a Sheikh, an old, old man and much I marvelled at their appearance and their all being blind in the same eye. When they saw me, they saluted me with the salaam and asked me of my case and my history, whereupon I related to them all what had befallen me and what full measure of misfortune was mine.

Marvelling at my tale, they took me to the mansion, where I saw ranged round the hall ten couches each with its blue bedding and coverlet of blue stuff and a-middlemost stood a smaller couch furnished like them with blue and nothing else.

As we entered each of the youths took his seat on his own couch and the old man seated himself upon the smaller one in the middle, saying to me, "O youth, sit thee down on the floor and ask not of our case, nor of the loss of our eyes."

Presently he rose up and set before each young man some meat in a charger and drink in a larger mazer, treating me in like manner and after that they sat questioning me concerning my adventures and what had betided me. And I kept telling them my tale until the night was far spent. Then said the young men, "O our Sheikh, wilt thou not set before us our ordinary? The time is come."

He replied, "With love and gladness," and rose and, entering a closet, disappeared, but presently returned bearing on his head ten trays each covered with a strip of blue stuff. He set a tray before each youth and, lighting ten wax candles, stuck one upon each tray and drew off the covers, and under them was naught but ashes and powdered charcoal and kettle soot.

Then all the young men tucked up their sleeves to their elbows and fell a-weeping and wailing and they blackened their faces and smeared their clothes and buffeted their brows and beat their breasts, continually exclaiming, "We were sitting at our ease, but our frowardness brought us unease!"

They ceased not to do thus until dawn drew nigh, when the old man rose and heated water for them and they washed their face and donned other and clean clothes. Now when I saw this for very wonderment my senses left me and my wits went wild and heart and head were full of thought, until I forgot what had betided me and I could not keep silence, feeling I had to speak out and question them of these strangeness.

So I said to them, "How come ye to do this after we have been so openhearted and frolicsome? Thanks be to Allah, ye be all sound and sane, yet actions such as these befit none but madmen or those possessed of an evil spirit. I conjure you by all that is dearest to you, why stint ye to tell me your history and the cause of losing your eyes and your blackening your faces with ashes and soot?"

Hereupon they turned to me and said, "O young man, hearken not to thy youthtide's suggestions and question us not."

Then they slept and I with them and when they awoke the old man brought us somewhat of food. And after we had eaten and the plates and goblets had been removed, they sat conversing until nightfall, when the old man rose and lit the wax candles and lamps and set meat and drink before us. After we had eaten and drunken we sat conversing and carousing in companionage until the noon of night, when they said to the old man, "Bring us our ordinary, for the hour of sleep is at hand!"

So he rose and brought them the trays of soot and ashes and they did as they had done on the preceding night, nor more, nor less. I abode with them after this fashion for the space of a month, during which time they used to blacken their faces with ashes every night and wash and change their raiment when the morn was young, and I but marvelled the more and my scruples and curiosity increased to such a point that I had to forgo even food and drink. At last I lost command of myself, for my heart was aflame with fire unquenchable and lowe unconcealable and I said, "O young men, will ye not relieve my trouble and acquaint me with the reason of thus blackening your faces and the meaning of your words, 'We were sitting at our ease, but our frowardness brought us unease'?"

Quoth they, "It would be better to keep these things secret."

Still I was bewildered by their doings to the point of abstaining from eating and drinking and at last wholly losing patience, quoth I to them, "There is no help for it. Ye must acquaint me with what is the reason of these doings."

They replied, "We kept our secret only for thy good. To gratify thee will bring down evil upon thee and thou wilt become a monocular even as we are."

I repeated, "There is no help for it and if ye will not, let me leave you and return to mine own people and be at rest from seeing these things, for the proverb saith, 'Better ye 'bide and I take my leave, for what eye sees not heart shall never grieve'."

Thereupon they said to me, "Remember, O youth, that should ill befall thee, we will not again harbour thee nor suffer thee to abide amongst us."

And bringing a ram, they slaughtered it and skinned it. Lastly they gave me a knife, saying, "Take this skin and stretch thyself upon it and we will sew it around thee. Presently there shall come to thee a certain bird - hight roc - that will catch thee up in its pounces and tower high in the air and then set thee down on a mountain. When thou feelest it is no longer flying, rip open the pelt with this blade and come out of it. The bird will be scared and will fly away and leave thee free. After this fare for half a day, the march will place thee at a palace wondrous fair to behold, towering high in the air and built of khalanj, lign aloes and sandalwood, plated with red gold and studded with all manner of emeralds and costly gems fit for seal rings. Enter it and thou shalt will to thy wish, for we have all entered that palace and such is the cause of our losing our eyes and of our blackening our faces. Were we now to tell thee our stories it would take too long a time, for each and every of us lost his left eye by an adventure of his own."

I rejoiced at their words and they did with me as they said and the bird roc bore me off and set me down on the mountain. Then I came out of the skin and walked on until I reached the palace. The door stood open as I entered and I found myself in a spacious and goodly hall, wide exceedingly, even as a horse course. And around it were a hundred chambers with doors of sandal and aloe woods plated with red gold and furnished with silver rings by way of knockers. At the head or upper end of the hall I saw forty damsels, sumptuously dressed and ornamented and one and all bright as moons. None could ever tire of gazing upon them and all so lovely that the most ascetic devotee on seeing them would become their slave and obey their will.

When they saw me the whole bevy came up to me and said, "Welcome and good cheer

to thee, O our lord! This whole month have we been expecting thee. Praised be Allah who hath sent us one who is worthy of us, even as we are worthy of him!"

Then they made me sit down upon a high divan and said to me, "This day thou art our lord and master and we are thy servants and thy handmaids, so order us as thou wilt." And I marvelled at their case. Presently one of them arose and set meat before me and I ate and they ate with me whilst others warmed water and washed my hands and feet and changed my clothes and others made ready sherbets and gave us to drink and all gathered around me, being full of joy and gladness at my coming. Then they sat down and conversed with me until nightfall, when five of them arose and laid the trays and spread them with flowers and fragrant herbs and fruits, fresh and dried and confections in profusion. At last they brought out a fine wine service with rich old wine and we sat down to drink, and some sang songs and others played the lute and psaltery and recorders and other instruments, and the bowl went merrily round.

Hereupon such gladness possessed me that I forgot the sorrows of the world one and all and said, "This is indeed life. O sad that 'tis fleeting!"

I enjoyed their company until the time came for rest and our heads were all warm with

wine, when they said, "O our lord, choose from amongst us her who shall be thy bedfellow this night and not lie with thee again until forty days be past."

So I chose a girl fair of face and perfect in shape, with eyes kohl-edged by nature's hand, hair long and jet-black, with slightly parted teeth and joining brows. 'Twas as if she were some limber graceful branchlet or the slender stalk of sweet basil to amaze and to bewilder man's fancy, even as the poet said of such an one, "To even her with greeny bough were vain. Fool he who finds her beauties in the roe. When hath the roe those lively lovely limbs, or honey dews those lips alone bestow? Those eyne, soul piercing eyne, which slay with love, which bind the victim by their shafts laid low? My heart to second childhood they beguiled. No wonder, love sick-man again is child! And I repeated to her the maker's words who said, "None other charms but shine shall greet mine eyes, nor other image can my heart surprise. Thy love, my lady, captives all my thoughts and on that love I will die and I will arise."

So I lay with her that night. None fairer I ever knew. And when it was morning, the damsels carried me to the hammam bath and bathed me and robed me in fairest apparel. Then they served up food and we ate and drank and the cup went round until nightfall, when I chose from among them one fair of form and face, soft-sided and a model of grace, such a one as the poet described when he said, "On her fair bosom caskets twain I scanned, sealed fast with musk seals lovers to withstand. With arrowy glances stand on guard her eyes, whose shafts would shoot who dares put forth a hand."

With her I spent a most goodly night and, to be brief, O my mistress, I remained with them in all solace and delight of life, eating and drinking, conversing and carousing and every night lying with one or other of them.

But at the head of the New Year they came to me in tears and bade me farewell, weeping and crying out and clinging about me, whereat I wondered and said, "What may be the matter? Verily you break my heart!"

They exclaimed, "Would Heaven we had never known thee, for though we have companied with many, yet never saw we a pleasanter than thou or a more courteous." And they wept again.

"But tell me more clearly," asked I, "what causeth this weeping which maketh my gall bladder like to burst?"

And they answered, "O lord and master, it is severance which maketh us weep and thou and thou only art the cause of our tears. If thou hearken to us we need never be parted

and if thou hearken not we part forever, but our hearts tell us that thou wilt not listen
to our words and this is the cause of our tears and cries."

"Tell me how the case standeth."

"Know, O our lord, that we are the daughters of kings who have met here and have lived
together for years and once in every year we are perforce absent for forty days. And
afterward we return and abide here for the rest of the twelve months eating and drinking and taking our pleasure and enjoying delights. We are about to depart according to
our custom and we fear lest after we be gone thou contraire our charge and disobey our
injunctions. Here now we commit to thee the keys of the palace, which containeth forty
chambers and thou mayest open of these thirty and nine, but beware lest thou open the
fortieth door, for therein is that which shall separate us forever."

Quoth I, "Assuredly I will not open it if it contain the cause of severance from you."

Then one among them came up to me and falling on my neck wept and recited these
verses, "If time unite us after absent-while, the world harsh-frowning on our lot shall
smile, and if thy semblance deign adorn mine eyes, I'll pardon time past wrongs and
bygone guile."

And I recited the following, "When drew she near to bid adieu with her heart unstrung, while care and longing on that day her bosom wrung, wet pearls she wept and mine like red camelians rolled and, joined in sad riviere, around her neck they hung."

When I saw her weeping I said, "By Allah, I will never open that fortieth door, never and nowise!" and I bade her farewell. Thereupon all departed flying away like birds, signalling with their hands farewells as they went and leaving me alone in the palace.

When evening drew near I opened the door of the first chamber and entering it found myself in a place like one of the pleasances of Paradise. It was a garden with trees of freshest green and ripe fruits of yellow sheen and its birds were singing clear and keen and rills ran wimpling through the fair terrene. The sight and sounds brought solace to my sprite and I walked among the trees and I smelt the breath of the flowers on the breeze and heard the birdies sing their melodies hymning the One, the Almighty, in sweetest litanies and I looked upon the apple whose hue is parcel red and parcel yellow, as said the poet, "Apple whose hue combines in union mellow my fair's red cheek, her hapless lover's yellow."

Then I looked upon the pear whose taste surpasseth sherbet and sugar and the apricot whose beauty striketh the eye with admiration, as if it were a polished ruby. Then I went out of the place and locked the door as it was before. When it was the morrow I opened the second door and entering found myself in a spacious plain set with tall date palms and watered by a running stream whose banks were shrubbed with bushes of rose and jasmine, while privet and eglantine, oxeye, violet and lily, narcissus, origane and the winter gilliflower carpeted the borders. And the breath of the breeze swept over these sweet-smelling growths diffusing their delicious odours right and left, perfuming the world and filling my soul with delight.

After taking my pleasure there awhile I went from it and, having closed the door as it was before, opened the third door, wherein I saw a high open hall pargetted with particoloured marbles and pietra dura of price and other precious stones and hung with cages of sandalwood and eagle wood, full of birds which made sweet music, such as the "thousand-voiced" and the cushat, the merle, the turtledove and the Nubian ringdove. My heart was filled with pleasure thereby, my grief was dispelled and I slept in that aviary until dawn.

Then I unlocked the door of the fourth chamber and therein found a grand saloon with forty smaller chambers giving upon it. All their doors stood open, so I entered and found them full of pearls and jacinths and beryls and emeralds and corals and carbuncles and all manner of precious gems and jewels, such as tongue of man may not describe. My thought was stunned at the sight and I said to myself, "These be things methinks united which could not be found save in the treasuries of a King of Kings, nor could the monarchs of the world have collected the like of these!"

And my heart dilated and my sorrows ceased. "For," quoth I, "now verily am I the Monarch of the Age, since by Allah's grace this enormous wealth is mine and I have forty damsels under my hand, nor is there any to claim them save myself."

Then I gave not over opening place after place until nine and thirty days were passed and in that time I had entered every chamber except that one whose door the Princesses had charged me not to open.

But my thoughts, O my mistress, ever ran on that forbidden fortieth and Satan urged me to open it for my own undoing, nor had I patience to forbear, albeit there wanted of the trusting time but a single day. So I stood before the chamber aforesaid and, after a moment's hesitation, opened the door, which was plated with red gold and entered.

I was met by a perfume whose like I had never before smelt and so sharp and subtle was the odour that it made my senses drunken as with strong wine and I fell to the ground in a fainting fit which lasted a full hour. When I came to myself I strengthened my heart and entering, found myself in a chamber whose floor was bespread with saffron and blazing with light from branched candelabra of gold and lamps fed with costly oils, which diffused the scent of musk and ambergris. I saw there also two great censers each big as a mazer bowl, flaming with lign aloes, nadd perfume, ambergris and honeyed scents and the place was full of their fragrance.

Presently I espied a noble steed, black as the murks of night when murkiest, standing ready saddled and bridled with a saddle of red gold before two mangers, one of clear crystal wherein was husked sesame and the other also of crystal containing water of the rose scented with musk. When I saw this I marvelled and said to myself, "Doubtless in this animal must be some wondrous mystery."

And Satan cozened me so I led him without the palace and mounted him, but he would not stir from his place. So I hammered his sides with my heels, but he moved not and then I took the rein whip and struck him withal. When he felt the blow, he neighed a neigh with a sound like deafening thunder and, opening a pair of wings, flew up with me in the firmament of heaven far beyond the eyesight of man. After a full hour of flight

171

172

he descended and alighted on a terrace roof and shaking me off his back, lashed me on the face with his tad and gouged out my left eye, causing it to roll along my cheek. Then he flew away.

I went down from the terrace and found myself again amongst the ten one-eyed youths sitting upon their ten couches with blue covers, and they cried out when they saw me, "No welcome to thee, nor aught of good cheer! We all lived of lives the happiest and we ate and drank of the best. Upon brocades and cloths of gold we took our rest and we slept with our heads on beauty's breast, but we could not await one day to gain the delights of a year!"

Quoth I, "Behold, I have become one like unto you and now I would have you bring me a tray full of blackness, wherewith to blacken my face and receive me into your society."

"No, by Allah," quoth they, "thou shalt not sojourn with us and now get thee hence!"

So they drove me away. Finding them reject me thus, I foresaw that matters would go hard with me and I remembered the many miseries which destiny had written upon my forehead and I fared forth from among them heavy-hearted and tearful-eyed, repeating to myself these words, "I was sitting at mine ease, but my frowardness brought me to unease."

Then I shaved beard and mustachios and eyebrows, renouncing the world and wandered in Kalandar garb about Allah's earth and the Almighty decreed safety for me until I arrived at Baghdad, which was on the evening of this very night.

Here I met these two other Kalandars standing bewildered, so I saluted them saying, "I am a stranger!" and they answered, "And we likewise be strangers!"

By the freak of fortune we were like to like, three Kalandars and three monoculars all blind of the left eye. Such is the cause of the shearing of my beard and the manner of my losing an eye.

The Angel of Death with the Proud and the Devout Man

Illustrated by Lee Misenheimer

It is related that one of the olden monarchs was once minded to ride out in state with the officers of his realm and the grandees of his retinue and display to the people the marvels of his magnificence.

So he ordered his Lords and Emirs to equip them therefore and commanded his keeper of the wardrobe to bring him the richest of raiment, such as befitted a King in his state and he bade them to bring his steeds of the finest breeds and pedigrees. Which being done, he chose out of the raiment what rejoiced him most and of the horses that which he deemed best and donning the clothes, mounted and set forth in state, making his destrier prance and curvet among his troops and glorying in his pride and despotic power.

And Iblis came to him and, laying his hand upon his nose, blew into his nostrils the breath of hauteur and conceit, so that he magnified and glorified himself and said in his heart, "Who among men is like unto me?"

And he became so arrogant and so taken up with the thought of his own splendour and magnificence, that he would not vouchsafe a glance to any man.

Presently there stood before him one clad in tattered clothes and saluted him, but he returned not his salaam, whereupon the stranger laid hold of his horse's bridle.

"Lift thy hand!" cried the King. "Thou knowest not whose bridle rein it is whereof thou takest hold."

Quoth the other, "I have a need of thee."

Quoth the King, "Wait until I alight and then name thy need."

Rejoined the stranger, "It is a secret and I will not tell it but in thine ear."

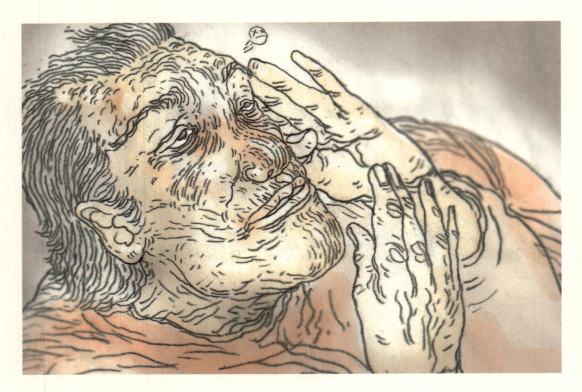

So the King bowed his head to him and he said, "I am the Angel of Death and I purpose to take thy soul."

Replied the King, "Have patience with me a little, whilst I return to my house and take leave of my people and children and neighbours and wife."

"By no means so," answered the Angel. "Thou shalt never return nor look on them again, for the fated term of thy life is past."

So saying, he took the soul of the King, who fell off his horse dead, and departed thence.

Presently the Angel of Death met a devout man, of whom Almighty Allah had accepted and saluted him. He returned the salute and the Angel said to him, "O pious man, I have a need of thee which must be kept secret."

"Tell it in my ear," quoth the devotee and quoth the other, "I am the Angel of Death."

Replied the man, "Welcome to thee! And praised be Allah for thy coming!"

Said the Angel, "If thou have any business, make an end of it," but the other answered, "There is nothing so urgent to me as meeting with my Lord."

And the Angel said, "How wouldst thou fain have me take thy soul? I am bidden to take it as thou willest and choosest."

176

He replied, "Tarry until I make the Wuzu ablution and pray and when I prostrate myself, then take my soul while my body is on the ground."

Quoth the Angel, "Verily, my Lord commanded me not to take thy soul but with thy consent and as thou shouldst wish, so I will do thy will."

Then the devout man made the minor ablution and prayed and the Angel of Death took his soul in the act of prostration and Almighty Allah transported it to the place of mercy and acceptance and forgiveness.

The Tale of
the Ensorcelled Prince

Illustrated by Sophie Toulouse

Know then, O my lord, that my sire was King of this city and his name was Mahmud, entitled Lord of the Black Islands and owner of what are now these four mountains. He ruled threescore and ten years, after which he went to the mercy of the Lord and I reigned as Sultan in his stead. I took to wife my cousin, the daughter of my paternal uncle and she loved me with such abounding love that whenever I was absent she ate not and she drank not until she saw me again. She cohabited with me for five years until a certain day when she went forth to the hammam bath and I bade the cook hasten to get ready all requisites for our supper. And I entered this palace and lay down on the bed where I was wont to sleep and bade two damsels to fan my face, one sitting by my head and the other at my feet. But I was troubled and made restless by my wife's absence and could not sleep, for although my eyes were closed, my mind and thoughts were wide-awake.

Presently I heard the slave girl at my head say to her at my feet, "O Mas'udah, how miserable is our master and how wasted in his youth and the pity of his being so betrayed by our mistress, the accursed whore!"

The other replied, "Yes indeed. Allah curse all faithless women and adulterous! But the like of our master, with his fair gifts, deserveth something better than this harlot who lieth abroad every night."

Then quoth she who sat by my head, "Is our lord dumb or fit only for bubbling that he questioneth her not!" and quoth the other, "Fie on thee! Doth our lord know her ways, or doth she allow him his choice? Nay, more, doth she not drug every night the cup she giveth him to drink before sleeptime and putting bhang into it? So he sleepeth and wotteth not whither she goeth, nor what she doeth, but we know that after giving him

the drugged wine, she donneth her richest raiment and perfumeth herself and then she fareth out from him to be away until break of day. Then she cometh to him and burneth a pasuntile under his nose and he awaketh from his death-like sleep."

When I heard the slave girls' words, the light became black before my sight and I thought night would never fall.

Presently the daughter of my uncle came from the baths and they set the table for us and we ate and sat together a fair half-hour quaffing our wine, as was ever our wont. Then she called for the particular wine I used to drink before sleeping and reached me the cup, but, seeming to drink it according to my wont, I poured the contents into my bosom and, lying down, let her hear that I was asleep.

Then, behold, she cried, "Sleep out the night and never wake again! By Allah, I loathe thee and I loathe thy whole body and my soul turneth in disgust from cohabiting with thee and I see not the moment when Allah shall snatch away thy life!"

Then she rose and donned her fairest dress and perfumed her person and slung my sword over her shoulder and opening the gates of the palace, went her ill way. I rose and followed her as she left the palace and she threaded the streets until she came to the city gate, where she spoke words I understood not and the padlocks dropped of themselves as if broken and the gate leaves opened. She went forth, and I after her without her noticing aught, until she came at last to the outlying mounds and a reed fence built about a round-roofed hut of mud bricks. As she entered the door, I climbed upon the roof, which commanded a view of the interior, and my fair cousin had gone in to a black slave. He was also a leper and a paralytic, lying upon a strew of sugar-cane trash and wrapped in an old blanket and the foulest rags and tatters. She kissed the earth before him and he raised his head so as to see her and said, "Woe to thee! What call hadst thou to stay away all this time? Here have been with me sundry of the black brethren, who drank their wine and each had his young lady and I was not content to drink because of thine absence."

Then she, "O my lord, my heart's love, knowest thou not that I am married to my cousin, whose very look I loathe and I hate myself when in his company? And did not I fear for thy sake, I would not let a single sun arise before making his city a ruined heap wherein raven should croak and howlet hoot and jackal and wolf harbour."

Rejoined the slave, "Thou liest, damn thee! Now I swear an oath by the valour and honour of black men, from today forth if thou stay away until this hour, I will not keep

company with thee nor will I glue my body with thy body. Dost play fast and loose with us, thou cracked pot, that we may satisfy thy dirty lusts, O vilest of the vile whites?"

When I heard his words and saw with my own eyes what passed between these two wretches, the world waxed dark before my face and my soul knew not in what place it was. But my wife humbly stood up weeping before and wheedling the slave, saying, "O my beloved and very fruit of my heart, there is none left to cheer me but thy dear self and, if thou cast me off, who shall take me in, O my beloved, O light of my eyes?"

And she ceased not weeping and abasing herself to him until he deigned be reconciled with her. Then was she right glad and stood up and doffed her clothes, even to her petticoat trousers and said, "O my master, what hast thou here for thy handmaiden to eat?" "Uncover the basin," he grumbled, "and thou shalt find at the bottom the broiled bones of some rats we dined on. Pick at them and then go to that slop pot, where thou shalt find some leavings of beer which thou mayest drink."

So she ate and drank and washed her hands and went and lay down by the side of the slave upon the cane trash and crept in with him under his foul coverlet and his rags and tatters.

When I saw my wife, my cousin, the daughter of my uncle, do this deed, I clean lost my wits and climbing down from the roof, I entered and took the sword which she had with her and drew it, determined to cut down the twain. I first struck at the slave's neck and thought that the death decree had fallen on him, for he groaned a loud hissing groan, but I had cut only the skin and flesh of the gullet and the two arteries! It awoke the daughter of my uncle, so I sheathed the sword and fared forth for the city and entering the palace, lay upon my bed and slept until morning, when my wife aroused me and I saw that she had cut off her hair and had donned mourning garments. Quoth she, "O son of my uncle, blame me not for what I do. It hath just reached me that my mother is dead and my father hath been killed in holy war and of my brothers one hath lost his life by a snake sting and the other by falling down some precipice and I can and should do naught save weep and lament."

When I heard her words I refrained from all reproach and said only, "Do as thou list. I certainly will not thwart thee."

She continued sorrowing, weeping and wailing one whole year from the beginning of its circle to the end and when it was finished she said to me, "I wish to build me in thy palace a tomb with a cupola, which I will set apart for my mourning and will name the House of Lamentations."

Quoth I again, "Do as thou list!"

Then she built for herself a cenotaph wherein to mourn and set on its centre a dome under which showed a tomb like a santon's sepulchre. Thither she carried the slave and lodged him, but he was exceedingly weak by reason of his wound and unable to do her love service. He could only drink wine and from the day of his hurt he spoke not a word, yet he lived on because his appointed hour was not come. Every day, morning and evening, my wife went to him and wept and wailed over him and gave him wine and strong soups and left not off doing after this manner a second year. And I bore with her patiently and paid no heed to her.

One day, however, I went in to her unawares and I found her weeping and beating her face and crying, "Why art thou absent from my sight, O my heart's delight? Speak to me, O my life, talk with me, O my love."

When she had ended for a time her words and her weeping I said to her, "O my cousin, let this thy mourning suffice, for in pouring forth tears there is little profit!"

"Thwart me not," answered she, "in aught I do, or I will lay violent hands on myself!"

So I held my peace and left her to go her own way and she ceased not to cry and keen and indulge her affliction for yet another year. At the end of the third year I waxed aweary of this longsome mourning and one day I happened to enter the cenotaph when vexed and angry with some matter which had thwarted me and suddenly I heard her say, "O my lord, I never hear thee vouchsafe a single word to me! Why dost thou not answer me O my master?" and she began reciting, "O thou tomb! O thou tomb! Be his beauty set in shade? Hast thou darkened that countenance all-sheeny as the noon? O thou tomb! Neither earth nor yet Heaven art to me, then how cometh it in thee are conjoined my sun and moon?"

When I heard such verses as these rage was heaped upon my rage, I cried out, "Wellaway! How long is this sorrow to last?" and I began repeating, "O thou tomb! O thou tomb! Be his horrors set in blight? Hast thou darkened his countenance that sickeneth the soul? O thou tomb! Neither cesspool nor pigskin art to me, then how cometh it in thee are conjoined soil and coal?"

When she heard my words she sprang to her feet crying, "Fie upon thee, thou cur! All this is of thy doings. Thou hast wounded my heart's darling and thereby worked me sore woe and thou hast wasted his youth so that these three years he hath lain abed more dead than alive!" In my wrath I cried, "O thou foulest of harlots and filthiest of whores! Yes, indeed it was I who did this good deed." And snatching up my sword, I drew it and made at her to cut her down. But she laughed my words and mine intent to scorn, crying, "To heel, hound that thou art! Alas for the past which shall no more come to pass, nor shall anyone avail the dead to raise. Allah hath indeed now given into my hand him who did to me this thing, a deed that hath burned my heart with a fire which died not a flame which might not be quenched!"

Then she stood up and pronouncing some words to me unintelligible, she said, "By virtue of my egromancy become thou half stone and half man!"

Whereupon I became what thou seest, unable to rise or to sit and neither dead nor alive. Moreover, she ensorcelled the city with all its streets and garths and she turned by her gramarye the four islands into four mountains around the tarn whereof thou questionest me. And the citizens, who were of four different faiths, Moslem, Nazarene, Jew and Magian, she transformed by her enchantments into fish. The Moslems are white, the Magians red, the Christians blue and the Jews yellow. And every day she tortureth me and scourgeth me with a hundred stripes, each of which draweth floods of blood and cutteth the skin of my shoulders to strips. And lastly she clotheth my upper half with

185

a haircloth and then throweth over them these robes. Hereupon the young man again shed tears and began reciting, "In patience, O my God, I endure my lot and fate, I will bear at will of Thee whatsoever be my state. They oppress me, they torture me, they make my life a woe, yet haply Heaven's happiness shall compensate my strait. Yea, straitened is my life by the bane and hate of foes, but Mustafa and Murtaza shall open me Heaven's gate."

After this the Sultan turned toward the young Prince and said, "O youth, thou hast removed one grief only to add another grief. But now, O my friend, where is she and where is the mausoleum wherein lieth the wounded slave?"

"The slave lieth under yon dome," quoth the young man, "and she sitteth in the chamber fronting yonder door. And every day at sunrise she cometh forth, and first strippeth and whippeth me with a hundred strokes of the leathern scourge and I weep and shriek, but there is no power of motion in my lower limbs to keep her off me. After ending her tormenting me she visiteth the slave, bringing him wine and boiled meats. And tomorrow at an early hour she will be here."

Quoth the King, "By Allah, O youth, I will assuredly do thee a good deed which the world shall not willingly let die, an act of derring-do which shall be chronicled long after I am dead and gone by."

Then the King sat him by the side of the young Prince and talked until nightfall, when he lay down and slept. But as soon as the false dawn showed, he arose and, doffing his outer garments, bared his blade and hastened to the place wherein lay the slave. Then was he ware of lighted candles and lamps and the perfume of incenses and unguents and directed by these, he made for the slave and struck him one stroke, killing him on the spot. After which he lifted him on his back and threw him into a well that was in the palace. Presently he returned and, donning the slave's gear, lay down at length within the mausoleum with the drawn sword laid close to and along his side. After an hour or so the accursed witch came and first going to her husband, she stripped off his clothes and, taking a whip, flogged him cruelly while he cried out, "Ah! Enough for me the case I am in! Take pity on me, O my cousin!"

But she replied, "Didst thou take pity on me and spare the life of my truelove on whom I doted?"

Then she drew the cilice over his raw and bleeding skin and threw the robe upon all and went down to the slave with a goblet of wine and a bowl of meat broth in her hands. She entered under the dome weeping and wailing, "Wellaway!" and crying, "O my lord! Speak a word to me! O my master! Talk awhile with me!" and began to recite these couplets,

"How long this harshness, this unlove, shall bide? Suffice thee not tear floods thou hast espied? Thou dost prolong our parting purposely and if wouldst please my foe, thou'rt satisfied!"

Then she wept again and said, "O my lord! Speak to me, talk with me!"

The King lowered his voice and, twisting his tongue, spoke after the fashion of the black slaves and said, "'Lack, 'lack! There be no Majesty and there be no Might save in Allah, the Glorious, the Great!"

Now when she heard these words she shouted for joy and fell to the ground fainting and when her senses returned she asked, "O my lord, can it be true that thou hast power of speech?" And the King, making his voice small and faint, answered, "O my cuss! Dost thou deserve that I talk to thee and speak with thee?"

"Why and wherefore?" rejoined she and he replied, "The why is that all the livelong day thou tormentest thy husband and he keeps calling on 'eaven for aid until sleep is strange to me even from evenin' until mawnin' and he prays and damns, cussing us two, me and thee, causing me disquiet and much bother. Were this not so, I should long ago have got my health and it is this which prevents my answering thee."

Quoth she, "With thy leave I will release him from what spell is on him," and quoth the King, "Release him and let us have some rest!"

She cried, "To hear is to obey," and, going from the cenotaph to the palace, she took a metal bowl and filled it with water and spake over it certain words which made the contents bubble and boil as a caldron seetheth over the fire. With this she sprinkled her husband saying, "By virtue of the dread words I have spoken, if thou becamest thus by my spells, come forth out of that form into thine own former form."

And lo and behold! The young man shook and trembled, then he rose to his feet and, rejoicing at his deliverance, cried aloud, "I testify that there is no god but the God and in very truth Mohammed is His Apostle, whom Allah bless and keep!"

Then she said to him, "Go forth and return not hither, for if thou do I will surely slay thee." So he went from between her hands and she returned to the dome and, going down to the sepulcher, she said, "O my lord, come forth to me that I may look upon thee and thy goodliness!"

The King replied in faint low words, "What thing hast thou done? Thou hast rid me of the branch, but not of the root."

She asked, "O my darling! What is the root?"

And he answered, "Fie on thee, O my cuss! The people of this city and of the four islands every night when it is half-passed lift their heads from the tank in which thou hast turned them to fish and cry to Heaven and call down its anger on me and thee and this is the reason why my body is balked from health. Go at once and set them free, then come to me and take my hand and raise me up, for a little strength is already back in me."

When she heard the King's words, and she still supposed him to be the slave, she cried joyously, "O my master, on my head and on my eyes be thy command. Bismillah!"

So she sprang to her feet and, full of joy and gladness, ran down to the tarn and took a little of its water in the palm of her hand and spake over it words not to be understood and the fishes lifted their heads and stood up on the instant like men, the spell on the people of the city having been removed. What was the lake again became a crowded capital. The bazaars were thronged with people who bought and sold, each citizen was occupied with his own calling and the four hills became islands as they were whilom. Then the young woman, that wicked sorceress, returned to the King, and still thinking

he was the black slave, said to him, "O my love! Stretch forth thy honoured hand that I may assist thee to rise."

"Nearer to me," quoth the King in a faint and feigned tone.

She came close as to embrace him, when he took up the sword lying hid by his side and smote her across the breast, so that the point showed gleaming behind her back. Then he smote her a second time and cut her in twain and cast her to the ground in two halves. After which he fared forth and found the young man, now freed from the spell, awaiting him and gave him joy of his happy release while the Prince kissed his hand with abundant thanks. Quoth the King, "Wilt thou abide in this city or go with me to my capital?"

Quoth the youth, "O King of the Age, wettest thou not what journey is between thee and thy city?"

"Two days and a half," answered he, whereupon said the other, "If thou be sleeping, O King, awake! Between thee and thy city is a year's march for a well-girt walker and thou haddest not come hither in two days and a half save that the city was under enchantment. And I, O King, will never part from thee, not even for the twinkling of an eye."

The King rejoiced at his words and said, "Thanks be to Allah, who hath bestowed thee upon me! From this hour thou art my son and my only son, for that in all my life I have never been blessed with issue."

Thereupon they embraced and joyed with exceeding great joy. And, reaching the palace, the Prince who had been spellbound informed his lords and his grandees that he was about to visit the Holy Places as a pilgrim and bade them get ready all things necessary for the occasion. The preparations lasted ten days, after which he set out with the Sultan, whose heart burned in yearning for his city, whence he had been absent a whole twelve months. They journeyed with an escort of Mamelukes carrying all manners of precious gifts and rarities, nor stinted they wayfaring day and night for a full year until they approached the Sultan's capital and sent on messengers to announce their coming. Then the Vizir and the whole army came out to meet him in joy and gladness, for they had given up all hope of ever seeing their King and the troops kissed the ground before him and wished him joy of his safety. He entered and took seat upon his throne and the Minister came before him and, when acquainted with all that had befallen the young Prince, he congratulated him on his narrow escape. When order was restored throughout the land, the King gave largess to many of his people and said to the Vizir, "Hither the fisherman who brought us the fishes!"

So he sent for the man who had been the first cause of the city and the citizens being delivered from enchantment and when he came into the presence, the Sultan bestowed upon him a dress of honour and questioned him of his condition and whether he had children. The fisherman gave him to know that he had two daughters and a son, so the King sent for them and, taking one daughter to wife, gave the other to the young Prince and made the son his head treasurer. Furthermore, he invested his Vizir with the Sultanate of the City in the Black Islands whilom belonging to the young Prince and dispatched with him the escort of fifty armed slaves, together with dresses of honour for all the Emirs and grandees. The Vizir kissed hands and fared forth on his way, while the Sultan and the Prince abode at home in all the solace and the delight of life and the fisherman became the richest man of his age and his daughters wived with the Kings until death came to them.

The City of
Many-Columned Iram

Illustrated by Matthias Gephart

Ad the Greater had two sons, Shadid and Shaddad, who when their father died ruled conjointly in his stead, and there was no King of the Kings of the earth but was subject to them. After awhile Shadid died and his brother Shaddad reigned over the earth alone. Now he was fond of reading in antique books, and happening upon the description of the world to come and of Paradise with its pavilions and pileries and trees and fruits and so forth, his soul move him to build the like thereof in this world, after the fashion aforesaid.

Now under his hand were a hundred thousand kings, each ruling over a hundred thousand chiefs, commanding each a hundred thousand warriors, so he called these all before him and said to them, "I find in ancient books and annals a description of Paradise as it is to be in the next world, and I desire to build me its like in this world. Go ye forth therefore to the goodliest tract on earth and the most spacious, and build me there a city of gold and silver whose gravel shall be chrysolite and rubies and pearls, and for support of its vaults make pillars of jasper. Fill it with palaces whereon ye shall set galleries and balconies, and plant its lanes and thoroughfares with all manner of trees bearing yellow-ripe fruits, and make rivers to run through it in channels of gold and silver."

Whereat said one and all, "How are we able to do this thing thou hast commanded, and whence shall we get the chrysolites and rubies and pearls whereof thou speakest?"

Quoth he, "What! Weet ye not that the kings of the world are subject to me and under my hand; and that none therein dare gainsay my word?"

Answered they, "Yes, we know that."

Whereupon the King rejoined, "Fare ye then to the mines of chrysolites and rubies and pearls and gold and silver and collect their produce and gather together all of value that is in the world, and spare no pains and leave naught. Also take for me such of

these things as be in men's hands and let nothing escape you. Be diligent and beware of disobedience."

And thereupon he wrote letters to all the kings of the world and bade them gather together whatso of these things was in their subjects' hands, and get them to the mines of precious stones and metals and bring forth all that was therein, even from the abysses of the seas.

This they accomplished in the space of twenty years, for the number of rulers then reigning over the earth was three hundred and sixty kings. And Shaddad presently assembled from all lands and countries architects and engineers and men of art and labourers and handicraftsmen, who dispersed over the world and explored all the wastes and wolds and tracts and holds. At last they came to an uninhabited spot, a vast and fair open plain clear of sand hills and mountains, with founts flushing and rivers rushing, and they said, "This is the manner of place the King commanded us to seek and ordered us to find."

So they busied themselves in building the city even as bade them Shaddad, King of the whole earth in its length and breadth, leading the fountains in channels and laying the foundations after the prescribed fashion. Moreover, all the kings of earth's several reigns sent thither jewels and precious stones and pearls large and small and carnelian and refined gold and virgin silver upon camels by land and in great ships over the waters, and there came to the builders' hands of all these materials so great a quantity as may neither be told nor counted nor conceived.

So they laboured at the work three hundred years, and when they had brought it to end they went to King Shaddad and acquainted him therewith. Then said he, "Depart and make thereon an impregnable castle, rising and towering high in air, and build around it a thousand pavilions, each upon a thousand columns of chrysolite and ruby and vaulted with gold, that in each pavilion a Vizir may dwell."

So they returned forthwith and did this in other twenty years, after which they again presented themselves before King Shaddad and informed him of the accomplishment of his will. Then he commanded his Vizirs, who were a thousand in number, and his chief officers and such of his troops and others as he put trust in to prepare for departure and removal to Many-Columned Iram, in the suite and at the stirrup of Shaddad, son of Ad, King of the world, and he bade also such as he would of his women and his harem and of his handmaids and eunuchs to make them ready for the journey.

They spent twenty years in preparing for departure, at the end of which time Shaddad set out with his host, rejoicing in the attainment of his desire until there remained but one day's journey between him and Iram of the Pillars. Then Allah sent down on him and on the stubborn unbelievers with him a mighty rushing sound from the Heavens of His power, which destroyed them all with its vehement clamour, and neither Shaddad nor any of his company set eyes on the city. Moreover, Allah blotted out the road which led to the city and it stands in its stead unchanged until the Resurrection Day and the Hour of Judgment."

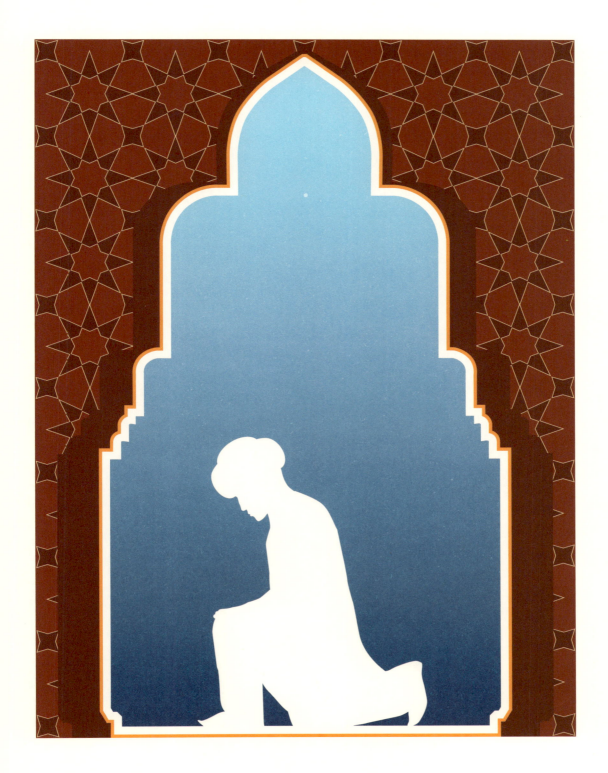

The Illustrators

Catalina Estrada Uribe
"Aladdin and the Wonderful Lamp"
Colombia, lives and works
in Barcelona, Spain.
katika@katika.net
www.katika.net

Cecilia Carlstedt
"The Fifth Voyage of
Sindbad the Seaman"
Sweden, lives and works
in Stockholm, Sweden.
mail@ceciliacarlstedt.com
www.agentform.se

Dr. Alderete & El Valiente
"The Third Voyage of
Sindbad the Seaman"
Mexiko, lives and works
in Mexico City, Mexico.
contacto@jorgealderete.com
www.jorgealderete.com
www.zoveck.com

Ella Tjader
"The Sweep and the Noble lady"
Lithuania, lives and works
in Glasgow, Scotland.
contact@artlaundry.com
www.artlaundry.com

Jens Harder
"The Man who stole the Dish of Gold
wherin the Dog ate"
Germany, lives and works
in Berlin, Germany.
jens@monogatari.de
www.monogatari.de

Jules Langran
"The Fouth Voyage of
Sindbad the Seaman"
England, lives and works
in Lewes, England.
me@jules.net
www.jules.net

Julia Pfaller
"The Second Voyage of
Sindbad the Seaman"
Germany, lives and works
in Berlin, Germany.
jp@juliapfaller.de
www.juliapfaller.de

Katharina Leuzinger
"The Tale of the Three Apples"
Switzerland, lives and works
in London, England.
katleuzinger@tiscali.co.uk
www.katleuzinger.com

Kate Sutton

"The Sixth Voyage of
Sindbad the Seaman"
England, lives and works
in Southport, England.
kate@sleepycow.com
www.sleepycow.com

Lee Misenheimer

"The Angel of Death with the
Proud and the Devout Man"
USA, lives and works
in New York, USA.
lee@destroyrockcity.com
www.destroyrockcity.com

Luise Vormittag &
Nicola Carter

"Sindbad the seaman"
Austria & England, lives and
works in London, England.
info@container.me.uk
www.container.me.uk

Mads Berg

"The Seventh Voyage of
Sindbad the Seaman"
Denmark, lives and works
in Copenhavn, Denmark.
post@madsberg.dk
www.madsberg.dk

Matthias Gephart

"The City of Many-Columned Iram"
Germany, lives and works
in Dortmund, Germany.
info@disturbanity.com
www.disturbanity.com

Pipa

"The Third Kalandar's Tale"
Brasil, lives and works
in London, England.
pipa@epwww.com
www.epwww.com

Simone Legno

„The First Voyage of
Sindbad the Seaman"
Italy, lives and works
in Los Angeles, USA.
simone@tokidoki.it
www.tokidoki.it

Sophie Toulouse

"The Tale of the Ensorcelled Prince"
France, lives and works
in Paris, France.
nationofangela@mac.com
www.sophietoulouse.com

1001 Nights – The Illustrated Fairy Tales from One Thousand and One Nights

Edited by Robert Klanten and Hendrik Hellige
Layout/Project Management: Hendrik Hellige
Proofreading: Ashley Marc Slapp
Production Management: Vinzenz Geppert
Cover- & Intro-Illustrations: Hendrik Hellige
Logotypeface based on the font "Orient"
by Wolfgang Rosenthal, www.i-o-n.de/font available at www.volcano-type.de

Printed in Germany

Bibliographic information published by Die Deutsche Bibliothek.
Die Deutsche Bibliothek lists this publication in the Deutsche Nationalbibliografie;
detailed bibliographic data is available in the Internet at http://dnb.ddb.de.

ISBN 3-89955-094-3